MW01290072

Daycare Whisperer™ Doing Daycare

This Job would be Great if it wasn't for the Parents!

Photography and cover design by Angel Blanchard.

A very special thank you to our cover models:
Jordan, Melinda and Kayci

To Vera Arlene Fees Carlson…

My auntie, my mother, my sister, my best friend.

This one's for you…

- Tori

And, to Mary Angeline Brierly…

You taught me how to be the woman I am today.

Until we meet again…

- Angel

Table of Contents

Meet the Daycare Whisperer

I have been a childcare provider for thirty-six years as a nanny, school nurse, and for the last twenty years, home childcare provider. As the years turned into decades, I have taught myself how to filter through the available prospective parents and choose the cream of the crop. The ability to choose the right customers is as important to the business as the skill set needed to provide excellent care to the children.

This book describes many types of parents I have worked with and learned about in my consulting business as the Daycare Whisperer. I have spent 16 years on childcare forums devouring life experience from my peers and engaging in conversations about their clients on the internet and in phone consultations. My own population of daycare children was about 65 children with approximately 110 parents. I operated a twenty-four hour daycare for well over a decade, serving two daily shifts of children and parents. My turnover rate was very low so my total population was smaller than most home childcares over the same time period.

I got the internet in 1998 and immediately joined a childcare forum. It was called Rainbow Room and looked a lot like Craigslist does now. It was not fancy and took a bit of time to get through, but it was communication with other providers. Hallelujah!!!!!!! I fell crazy in love with the boards. The isolation I felt as an in-home, self-employed worker was lifted. For the first time since I opened up shop, I had a chance to have co-workers and mentors. The women I met on the boards sixteen years ago are still on the internet with me! Now we are on Facebook together and do not use usernames. We know each other by our real names and at the touch of a screen I can reach all of them. If you are a provider and would like to join this large group of veteran providers, send me a friend request on the Daycare Whisperer Facebook page and I will hook you up!

I post on daycare.com and ivillage under my username, Nannyde. In the archives you can read over ten thousand of my posts spanning the last sixteen years. I also have a blog on daycare.com called, "Nannyde the Daycare Whisperer."

I adore daycare.com. It is the most amazing childcare forum with a treasure trove of childcare information, a slamming archive and an easy search engine. I am forever grateful to Michael Castello, owner of daycare.com, for developing such an amazing and simple site. He gave me my first childcare provider writing job (Daycare.com presents Nannyde the Daycare Whisperer) and has been my mentor as I developed my Daycare Whisperer consulting business.

If you have not had the pleasure of joining daycare.com I highly encourage you to bop on over there and have a look-see. You will find an amazing group of providers from newbies to veterans. The traffic is phenomenal and the number of active users is the highest I have seen in 16 years on the boards. Michael is a phenomenal leader and is completely involved in the day-to-day business of the board. My good buddy, Christa Mostoller, is the moderator and leader of the board. She is a veteran provider with a skillset like none other. Whether you are a parent or provider, please take a bit of time and checkout daycare.com.

From the first time I hopped on the internet, I used it like a big encyclopedia and started researching all things child. To this day, the majority of my free time is spent researching every aspect of childcare and current research on health and safety. I have been able to combine three and a half decades of direct care of children, operating a business and tens of thousands of hours of research to establish the Daycare Whisperer consulting business to offer expert services for home childcare providers, centers, human service workers and expert witness for criminal and civil cases for child injury and death in childcare.

This book in the Doing Daycare series is about parent behavior and how to manage different parenting styles in the childcare business. Most of the information in this book will be about maladaptive and difficult parental behavior.

It is risky to shine a light on the darker side of childcare and even riskier to target the customers... the clients… the parents. I do not know of any childcare author who has devoted a book to specific types of parents. I hope this book and the following books in the Doing Daycare series will help new and veteran providers to cultivate and preserve the perfect daycare parent partnerships.

Dear Parents...

Today is the first day of the rest of your life and the last day at my house. Your children are the worst behaved children I have ever seen in my twenty-year career. The only people I know who are more badly behaved than your children are their parents.

Do not worry about calling the state. I already did. I hope they come and do your "retaliatory complaint" inspection while we are having your children's "gone away" party. I am having it catered and hiring a dog and pony show.

Speaking of dog and pony shows... I will not miss your drop-off performance of the academy award worthy "Mom Loves Baby" show. When you stand in my doorway in your pajama bottoms and oversized t-shirt professing how much you will miss your little Pookie and Snowflake, the irony is sadly laughable. Your 27th "ME" day this year COULD be spent with your children. I swear if tomorrow was the end of the world, your children would show up for daycare... Early.

I am terminating you because of your persistent attempts to bring them to my house doped up on fever masking drugs and subsequent refusal to answer your phone when the medication wears off. I cannot endure another moment of your foot stomping proclamation that you cannot miss another day of work to care for your own sick kids.

I am terminating you because I cannot sit in the front row and lay witness to their violence toward you. I cannot keep my anger in check when I watch them slap, punch, claw, bite, kick and spit at you when you beg them to do something as simple as putting on their shoes or getting into the car seat. I am worn down by the ridiculous excuses you make. They are not tired or suffering from allergies or teething. They are not bored because I am not honoring or serving their giftedness. They are out of control because you allow it without consequence. You either do not know how to discipline them or you do not want them to cry. I am leaning toward the latter.

Finally, I am terminating your family because of the absence of respect from the lot of you. I will not be called a bitch in my own home, especially by a three-year old. I will not be treated like an employee when I am self-employed.

I want money, but I don't want yours.

Do not try to sway me to change my mind. Do not try to apologize now and promise to address the concerns you shunned so readily yesterday so you can have daycare tomorrow. I will not take your children back or care for any future children you bring into this unsuspecting world. I will not care for your friends, acquaintances or any blood relative within the fourth degree of consanguinity.

You have taken five years of my happiness I cannot get back. The only thing I have left to give is your year-end receipt and the termination letter I should have been brave enough to give you years ago.

Be gone!

Your Childcare Provider

Well, I feel better. Don't you? Haven't we all been to the point where we wish we could lash out with how we really feel?

This letter is fictitious but was wickedly fun to write. I have not personally dealt with a family with all the issues of this family, but I think we could all relate to at least some aspects of their story.

Wouldn't it be great to be able to give a parent this kind of termination letter? It is a far cry from the ones we usually give out.

The standard termination letter goes something like this:

Dear Parent,

It has been an honor to care for your beautiful children, Pookie and Snowflake. I am saddened to inform you that my program no longer meets their needs. Please let this serve as our agreed upon two-week notice of termination. Should you find care before the end of the two weeks, please feel free to start as soon as it is convenient for your family.

Respectfully,

Your Provider

How we choose to let parents know we will no longer work for them is not anywhere near as important as what happened to get us to that point in the first place. What leads a daycare relationship to end so badly? What causes a provider to accept terrible parent and child behavior for months and even years?

This book is written to specifically discuss recalcitrant parental behavior. It is not a reflection of all parents, but rather the parents whose unseemly behavior stresses the provider and taints her ability to do her job well and be prosperous in her career.

It is my hope that within these pages providers at all levels of experience and education can find useful information and tools to recognize and deal with troublesome parents.

The Superb, Outstanding, Exceptional, Marvelous, Wonderful, Magnificent Parent

Before we begin the journey to the dark side of daycare parents, I want to tell you about the superb, outstanding, exceptional, marvelous, wonderful, magnificent parent…

Six years ago I met a family who had recently had their first born. They had already hired a babysitter for their cute and amazingly furry, little spud muffin, but they had seen an advertisement for my business and decided to interview with me just in case the provider they chose did not workout. When they arrived at my home for the first of three interviews, I watched them get out of their car. They were both smiling with the kind of smile that says, "I am SO happy to meet you" and I was immediately put at ease. I could just feel they were genuine human beings. They were the type of people you wish were in your immediate family.

They sat on my couch and we had a perfect interview. The mom was a preschool teacher and the dad was a food inspector. They were brilliant and funny and the questions they asked did not come from a book or a blog. They came up with their own questions and each was excellent. I could not have prepared for that interview if I had tried. I was so gobsmacked by their knowledge of children and group care.

This first interview went so well, I was actually sad when it was time for them to go home. When they were going out the door they gave me a hug. That was the only hug I ever received on a first meeting. When the Dad started down my sidewalk he turned and gave me a smile as big as Texas and nodded his head. I knew. He knew. Mom knew. This was a match.

I do three interviews. The first one is a "get to know you" meeting. I do not go too far into the policies of the business the first time I meet prospective clients because I just want to get a feel for who they are and if we will be able to communicate and work together. I normally hate interviewing because I do not have to do it too often and I am always out of practice by the time I have an opening. I enjoyed every minute I had with this lovely couple. I could have had them move in that day!

Much to my benefit, their initial provider did not work out. We had two more interviews and the parents signed on. I got to see the floppy, little, newborn bundle of sweetness on every visit. Before they actually started bringing the baby to daycare, the baby's grandmother from Kenya came to visit. She decided to stay for six weeks and kept the baby home with her.

When a parent has a chance to get free childcare for six weeks they normally ask the provider for a concession to keep the slot for free or for a reduced rate. This family did not even ask. They gladly paid me for six weeks. They knew I had to have income for the slot and they did not want to lose it.

They began care mid-November, right before the four-day Thanksgiving weekend and my two-week vacation at Christmas. They did not baulk about paying my fee despite the fact they paid for six weeks, but only had three weeks of care. They agreed to the fee when they signed on and it never once came up.

When their little boy was nearly one, I made the single biggest mistake I have ever made in my career with their little boy. My mistake could have caused injury or even death. It took me a few hours to figure out what I had done. The mom came to pick the baby up and with tears flowing down my cheeks I told her the mistake I had made. I was so scared and devastated that I could have harmed him. I offered to pay for immediate medical care so he could be examined to make sure he was okay.

As I cried the ugly cry, she gave me the biggest hug and said it would be okay. We decided to keep a vigil on him and if anything went even slightly sideways we would get him to the doctor. Luckily, the mistake I made did not affect him at all. Absolutely nothing happened. It was a near miss, but a mistake none the less.

They had the right to pull him from me that day. They knew it was a pure mistake. There was no way I could have known the possibility this error could occur as I did not have the life experience to know it could. They forgave me instantly and were more worried about how torn up I was in making such a huge mistake then they were about his safety in my care.

As the years rolled on, the family bestowed upon me another beautiful, but very different, floppy-eared bundle of cute. He was a bit more of a challenge than the one who came before him and we had to work together a lot more than we were used to.

In the five years I worked for them we never had a single day when anything went unspoken. When we had issues we talked… and talked... and talked. We relied on each other for the truth.

I can count on one hand the times they were late in five years. Each time they paid me a ridiculous late fee and followed up with a cup of special coffee or some other deliciousness from the Quickie Mart the next morning. They gave me wonderful Christmas bonuses and every holiday they wrote me beautiful notes thanking me for the care of their boys. I kept them all.

When I decided to make a major change in my life and move a couple hours away, I had to inform these parents I was shutting down the daycare. These two awesome parents were sad but so kind and understanding. The day before we moved, they took me and my son and out for treats. I miss them with every cell in my body. As I type this I can barely hold back the tears; I think of their sons as my sons and I love them like they are my own flesh and blood. They recently added a beautiful, sweet, little love princess to the family. I admit I cried when I saw her first picture and had a moment of regret moving away from them. I try at least once a month to convince them to move north so I can have their children here with me. I have a dream of them having many more children (as in 19 kids and counting!) so I can be their private nanny. I miss them that much.

I could have picked many families I worked for in the last two decades to feature as the perfect parents. I am so fortunate to have had so many.

I picked these two parents because they embodied the hard work of an excellent parent-provider relationship. It is a marriage of sorts and they were committed to doing it right.

I picked them because of the many times money could have severed our relationship, but they did not choose money over the best Nan for their kids.

I picked them because in the darkest moment of my career they forgave and gave me another chance. They did not have to and I would not have blamed them if they didn't.

I picked them because we made it five years without a cross word between us, primarily because they never once took advantage of me.

I picked them because they love and respect me and my son.

This book is not about them or any of the other parents who have blessed my life and taught me how to perfect my craft. My success has come from being able to pick out the parents who are wonderful human beings and excellent parents. Their children are my heart and my life's work.

I cannot thank them enough.

Daycare Whispers...

When you work for parents who are excellent customers, tell them THANK YOU every single day.

Let the parents know how much you admire their children and compliment them on what excellent parents you believe them to be.

Tell the parents that you are learning from them how to be a better parent yourself and a better provider.

If you are going to do special for a parent, consider the excellent parent as the one who will receive special. They deserve it.

Keep in touch with these parents after they leave. They will be a blessing to your career far longer than the years you worked with them.

The "MyChild" Parent

A MyChild parent is a parent who has a grandiose perception of themselves as a parent, their child and their child's needs, their rights regarding the child and their abilities with their child. They pretend to worship at the altar of their child and expect the world to join them by sitting behind them with their hands clasped and eyes down.

The MyChild mother has an excessive preoccupation with her child insofar as it reflects her prowess as a parent. She has an idealized vision of herself as a nurturer. She easily directs the care of her child, but she resents the work that goes into childrearing and sees it as a burden. She is most comfortable delegating the care of the child and feels she is doing an excellent job as a parent, not by what she does, but what she arranges for her child. In the expectations of what to do with her child, she appears to be a Tiger Mom or Mama Bear. When issues arise in the care of her child, she demands whatever special consideration it takes to make her Pookie happy. She sees Pookie's happiness as a reflection of her parenting excellence.

The MyChild mindset begins to develop before the parents are even expecting a child. This parent clings to mantras such as… "If they did that to MyChild I would kill them; I will not allow MyChild to do this or that; That would never happen to MyChild." They believe they will control and protect the child by any means necessary.

This unborn fantasy child is an extension of the mother, someone who can be used to make her feel special and inspire others to admire her. She enjoys parenting before the child is born and will seize any opportunity to discuss her motherhood with shop clerks, medical professionals, and prospective childcare providers.

The MyChild mother often begins interviewing for child care shortly after she conceives. She does extensive research to learn the right questions to ask of prospective childcare providers. After the first interview, she realizes the childcare providers give her a unique kind of attention that the rest of the world does not. They talk to her about specific parenting wants and demands before she even gives birth. Her excuse for looking for care long before she needs it is because she has heard that infant slots are hard to find. She does extensive phone interviewing and web site reading to develop her MyChild portfolio and questionnaire. Her list of questions can be condensed into one major theme: "How much one-to-one care will MyChild get?"

Now, every new parent wants to make sure an adult can manage their child within the group of children, but the MyChild parent is not concerned about why the provider may or may not be able to do one-to-one care. She just wants a declaration the provider will. If the provider told this parent she would forsake the care of all others to ensure her baby would get the cream of the crop attention, the MyChild mother would not stop and think that this provider should not ignore the care of any child just for hers. She would not consider that this promise may have been given to the other baby's mothers, too. She is satisfied that after explaining what her child needs, the provider will deliver.

This parent interviews a legion of providers while she is pregnant. If the mother tells you she has interviewed twenty plus providers, be on red alert. You will give away hours of your free time and endure multiple texts and phone calls until this parent becomes bored with considering you or is required to put money down to continue with you. Your odds of landing the child are very low and if you do, you could be in for a bumpy ride.

One of the first signs the parent you have taken into your business is a MyChild parent is the MyChild letter that comes with the baby on the first day of care. This is a care manual for the baby. It does not matter if the provider is more experienced in childcare or even a veteran daycare provider. Nor does it matter if the provider has cared for the baby's older siblings since birth. The

MyChild mother believes she is the expert on her child and must instruct the provider how to care for the child.

Here is an example of a MyChild letter.

Instructions for Snowflake Smith:

Eating habits: Snow eats about 20 to 30 ounces per day from morning until bedtime. I will feed Snow his morning bottle before I bring him and if for some reason I cannot, I will let you know. Snow also drinks about one ounce of pear juice diluted with one to two ounces of water every day to help soften his bowel movements. I would like half of his bottles to be breast milk and half of them to be formula. I will leave it up to you when you would like to give him breast milk and when you want to give him formula. However, Snow has a much easier time digesting the breast milk than the formula.

Snowflake is also gassy and some days has a lot of spit up so make sure to burp him thoroughly or he will become very fussy and cranky. Some days he wants to eat more and some days less. It all depends, but in general, the following is his daily eating schedule:
9-930 am - 4 oz bottle
11:30 am - 4 oz bottle
4:00 pm - 4 oz bottle

Sleeping habits: Snowflake takes two long naps. The first one is the morning from about 8 am to 9:30 am. His second long nap is in the afternoon from 1:30 pm to 3:30 pm. He also takes smaller "cat naps" throughout the day, but these do not last very long, anywhere from 20 to 35 minutes.

Likes: The most important thing for Snowflake is to be held as much as you possibly can! This is what he likes the best: just being held and close to you. He also likes to be wrapped in a blanket with his arms out for comfort while he is falling asleep. His favorite is his green blanket, which I will bring for him to use. Snowflake also likes to be rocked in a rocking chair while he is eating his bottles. If he is upset he likes to have a pacifier and be rocked while you sing to him. He also likes to have his nose, cheeks and chin touched while you say, "Beep!" We usually play this game on the floor and it makes him smile and coo! He likes to grab your thumbs and fingers while you gently pull him up so he can sit up for a minute and then lay back down. He also likes to grab your fingers as you gently rock him from side to side while he's on the floor.

Dislikes: Snowflake does not like tummy time. We put him on his tummy for a few minutes at a time every day, but he gets upset and starts to snort because his face is mashed into the blanket. He will also get upset if there is a lot of yelling back and forth going on or if there are really loud noises coming out of nowhere. He HATES being put down for longer than 10-15 minutes or so and when left alone, he starts to get really sad. You can put him down next to you, but not away from you or the group. It will take some time to calm him down if these things happen.

Concerns: The main thing I am concerned about is that he will not get enough hugs, kisses or time to be held. He NEEDS this stuff!!!! He was born a snuggler who wants to be close to people AT ALL TIMES and I know it is hard because you have your hands full, but I just want him to feel loved and not alone because I am not there. I am also concerned that Pookie might be jealous of Snowflake at times because Snowflake NEEDS more attention than her and she might start acting out to get more attention. If this starts happening please let me know as soon as possible.

Sincerely,
Snowflake's Mama

Do you see what I see? At first blush, this letter sounds like a new mother whose heart is breaking because she has to put her newborn in childcare. She looks like a mother who wishes she could stay home and care for her baby.

I see it differently. There is more to the story.

This letter was written years ago by a mother who already had one child in childcare with the provider. This mother took three months off when the baby was born with one of those months being prior to birth. She was not ill or having complications. She sent her oldest daughter to childcare every single day during the month before the baby was born and every single day of her two-month maternity leave. She was given the offer of having the three months off unpaid at daycare for the oldest and guaranteed a slot for both children when she returned to work. She declined. She could have had a three-month maternity leave instead of a two-month leave, but she wanted time to herself before the baby was born.

During her maternity leave, the father took the older child to daycare every morning and picked her up every evening. This meant the older child was in care additional hours. The mom was caught doping the older child during an illness so she could send her to childcare. She was home with the baby but wanted the older child in daycare despite being sick. It was too much for her to care for them both at the same time. She also sent her baby to daycare sick when she and the older child were already at home ill with the same stomach virus. She did not have a problem sending a sick baby to daycare when she was already home.

The schedule she set for the baby eating was one that was convenient for her. Notice the two hours between two feedings and the four and a half hours between the next. The last feeding was to be given to the baby right before pick-up so she did not have to do a feeding when she walked in the door after work. The line about her doing the first feeding of the day "if she could" turned into a battle because she attempted to send the baby unfed and had to be told she MUST feed the baby before daycare.

The section on what the baby NEEDS because he was born that way is very typical in the MyChild letters. The mom professes how HER child needs one-to-one care and MUST have an adult right by the baby's side at all times. She gives a passing wave to the notion that there were other children in the daycare even though she actually knew they were also young infants. Her main concern about the other children was her own first born, not the other babies in the house.

There were a whole lot of special-special requests packed into one little letter for one little baby. Despite pleading her baby's case that he was "born that way" and he "NEEDS!" his own adult, she knew…

- the provider could not rock her baby to sleep and allow him to sleep right beside her (even if he would be "sad" if he was alone).
- she was paying for a slot in a group daycare with other infants.
- the provider is not allowed to use blankets for the baby.
- the provider does a significant amount of belly time every day with every baby.
- state laws prohibit a child being held while sleeping and sleeping anywhere other than a playpen or crib.
- the provider cannot give juice or water to a newborn.

She had an older child in daycare before this baby. She knew the ropes and she tried to impress upon the provider that her child was special and required special care. She was certain he would be upset because he missed her so much. She cried dramatically the first day she dropped off the child and called multiple times during the day to check on him.

That lasted one day.

What happened the first week of childcare may surprise you. The mom stopped breastfeeding and switched to all formula. The mom changed her hours at work so she would have a longer day. She took multiple days off once she did go back to work and did not keep either kid home. In the years after the child entered daycare, the mother did not keep the child home a SINGLE day she was not forced to. She took the older child out of preschool to spend time with her to go to the zoo and to the movies but the second child was in daycare every single day.

She requested the provider switch the child's nap after he turned a year old so that he was up early in the afternoon in order to go to bed earlier in the evening. Seven p.m. bedtime was cutting into her time with the older child. She did not get home until five p.m. and wanted the baby in bed two hours later.

I could give countless examples of how the mom who wrote the MyChild letter was not the same mom a week, month, year or three years later. The mom who sits on your couch bawling and professing her sadness over leaving her child in childcare is often the mom who does not want to be around the child once she goes back to work. The mom who writes the longest most specific, heart wrenching, MyChild letter is the one who shuns her child and diminishes her responsibility of care to words instead of actions.

Childcare providers are often confused about how much MyChild they should allow with each child in their daycare. The provider may be a MyChild parent herself. She may have chosen to do childcare so that she could completely raise her own children and avoid any interference with her own MyChild. Hosting another person's MyChild feels fraudulent because they reserve that sentiment for only their own. Allowing a disproportionate amount of MyChild care of a daycare child will interfere with the care of her own children and dramatically affect her ability to evenly disperse her attention amongst her charges.

One of the most incorrect notions a MyChild parent can have is "I know my baby best and I know what's best for my baby." Many childcare books and pediatricians promote this idea because it sells books and services. What more does a brand new mommy want to hear or read besides this propaganda? "You are the mother of the child. She is your flesh and blood. She grew inside of you for nine months. You know her like no one else ever can or ever will."

The problem is that this is not true. Having sex, conceiving and giving birth to a child do not make someone knowledgeable about the care of that newborn. Having experience with other newborns makes you knowledgeable about newborns. Having experience with many newborns makes you REALLY knowledgeable.

Now, I am not suggesting a parent does not understand their child in a familial way. Of course, we all have a tribal recognition of our relatives. We have more commonality with them than others in this world. We love our own people singularly. That is what has made us evolve.

It used to be that mothers would learn to mother by example. There were multi-generational family members around to teach the mothers how to care for other people's babies. There were multiple siblings and as the siblings had children each girl was expected to contribute to their care. Older sisters took care of younger siblings. As the female children aged, they had a higher likelihood and expectation to care for the younger ones. By the time they had their own child they had enough experience to understand the basics of baby care.

This dynamic is rare in today's world. Family generations live separately and the number of children in the household has decreased dramatically. It is entirely possible that today's mother hasn't had any actual hands on experience with children. She goes to books and the internet to learn how to care for her baby. The books say "you know your baby best" and the mom says, "right on."

This leads to a crisis of overconfidence. I had a mother of a three-month old tell me that she was a "gifted newbie mother." She spent her entire pregnancy researching parenting and by the time she had her baby, she had a wealth of information to parent a child. This was the same mom who worked ten to eleven hours a day and had a two-hour commute. She was away from her child twelve to thirteen hours a day.

Within all those articles and books she read, the one concept that did not make it into any chapter was how being good at parenting involves actually caring for your child when they are awake. I gladly let the family go because I grew tired of discussing how the baby kept the mom up all night long. I had to be the one to break it to her that the baby was going to get his mommy time in one way or the other. The eleven hours they were together was all that was available to him. If she wanted to sleep at night she had to spend time with him during the day.

The mom would send me articles about safety and infant growth and development. I would send back links to blogs and articles I wrote on the subject three years before she had her child. She did not even recognize a veteran provider when she had one caring for her kid. I know more about babies in my pinky then she will know in her entire motherhood. I am not bragging. I have been at it for 36 years. I should be great at it by now.

Childcare is the ONLY profession I know where the worker can have decades of multi-faceted, hands on experience and still be viewed as having less knowledge than a customer who has had one singular experience for a few days, weeks or months. The parent who believes they are more knowledgeable and more powerful because they are the parent can destroy a childcare business and threaten a childcare provider's livelihood, freedom and ability to raise her own children. Having a baby does NOT make a parent an expert in the field. They should be viewed as a new, inexperienced parent and their wishes for the care of their child should always be evaluated as to whether or not they are best for the baby, the business, the other children, the provider and the provider's family.

The MyChild parent may make requests for the care of their child that you cannot oblige because they are unsafe, unfair or uncompensated. I do not recommend going against the parent's wishes, but, rather, offering what you CAN do within your scope of practice and asking a parent if they would like that service. If the parent does not want the service you offer, they need to move on down the road.

A parent cannot give you permission to do the wrong thing. When a parent brings a child into society, society has a stake in the outcome of that child. There are laws that were made regarding that child before the parents even met. There are human service agencies and insurance companies that dictate some of what happens to the child while the child is with a provider. The parent does not and cannot decide everything for their child when the child is away from them.

When a parent puts their child into a car they are required to put the child in a car seat. They do not get to decide. When the parent pulls out of their driveway with their child in the car they come upon a stop sign at the end of the street. That stop sign is the law. It was put there before the baby was born. The parent cannot say "my baby is in the car and I do not want to stop." Just because they have a baby does not mean they get to decide EVERYTHING that happens to the baby. The only way they get to make this decision is if they do not take the baby out into society or they find a caregiver who provides the exact services they want.

The common MyChild requests that cannot be accommodated in a group of children or within the safety and minimum standards for childcare are:

- Scheduling opposite of the other children; i.e., baby being awake while the other kids are sleeping and vice-versa.
- Baby being held throughout their nap.
- Pacifier in mouth while baby is being rocked to sleep.
- Baby having bottle, cloth, special lovey or blankie in bed.
- Baby sleeping in swing.
- Baby sleeping on belly.
- Baby being carried in a wrap on the provider.
- No belly time because baby cries.
- Baby or child wearing jewelry. (i.e., amber teething necklaces for teething infants or earrings to avoid piercings closing)
- Special food.
- Baby food before six months.
- Baby food in a bottle.
- For babies under one-year: withholding formula and feeding baby food to fill them up.
- Special sippy cup because the baby or toddler will not drink out of anything else.

- Straws in glasses so baby can take one sip at a time.
- Feeding via syringe or dropper for breastfed babies who will not drink out of a bottle.
- Baby or toddler cannot be outside or baby or toddler must be outside.
- Potty training before the age of 18 months.
- Toys and household items from home.
- Medication to be given exclusively at daycare because child refuses at home.
- Coins allowed in child's pockets because child likes carrying coins.
- No restraining equipment. No high chairs: baby must be held while he is spoon fed. No exersaucers or jolly jumpers because child cannot be trapped. Child must run free at all times. No play yards at any time.
- Baby switched to whole milk before the age of one (so parents do not have to supply formula for daycare).
- Cloth diapers for daycare when child wears commercial diapers at home.
- Daily reports in writing.
- Daily food intake reports.
- Daily massage and lotion of child without a skin condition.
- Baby only sleeping in the proximity of the provider.
- Infant curriculum.
- Provider is never to use the word "no" with child.
- Child in underwear or naked when potty training.
- No TV or screens. (Parents only want the child on screens when they are home.)
- Stating child has "allergies" in order to control what they are fed by the provider.
- Prepare separate meals if Pookie does not like the food.

When a MyChild parent has made a request for services and the provider does not deliver, they often withdraw the child. They believe that as the parent, they should be able to dictate everything about the child's care. The most important aspect of working with these clients is to know your state regulations, best practice in health and safety and how much you can afford to offer the parent for the tuition they are paying.

You will not be protected from being cited by your state or prosecuted by the government because you were following a parent's directions when an accident or injury occurs. You will not be covered by your insurance if you knowingly do something that is dangerous or against best practice even if you have the parent's blessing.

Educating this parent on what you are legally able to do and what their payment actually covers is a painstaking process because it challenges their fundamental parental belief system. Their acceptance of your final word may be solely because they have unsuccessfully attempted to find other providers who will do as they are told. You may also find yourself put in the very uncomfortable position of having to turn the parent in for child neglect if you should become privy to information they are employing unsafe practices with their child despite being educated about the risk. The parent does not believe you or the government should tell them what they can do with the child.

Daycare Whispers…

The MyChild parent will often behave very differently after the baby begins care. The more dramatic the expectations and behavior of the parent are, the more that parent will shun the care of the child after the child enters care.

Be firm about what you can and cannot do with the child.

Parents cannot give you permission to do the wrong thing.

You must follow the parent's wishes when it comes to care, but you do not have to keep the child if the parent's wishes are the wrong thing to do.

Do not provide services to parents who request you to do anything that is uncompensated, unsafe or inappropriate for group care.

The Parental Attention Seeking Syndrome (PASS) Parent

There are different ways in which parents use the relationship with their childcare provider to garner attention for themselves. Since the provider wants the client's business, she will often tolerate a lot of unnecessary interactions with the parent. This is because she fears the client will not choose her or will withdraw her children from the childcare. Attempts to get the forced interactions down to a more reasonable toll on the provider's time and resources are often met with resistance or the parent develops another "in" to rekindle the same response as the other behaviors that have won her the attention of the provider.

During the first pregnancy, the mom receives a lot of attention. The medical community, family, friends and co-workers focus on the pregnant mother - especially when the mom becomes big enough to show. This attention is due to the excitement of a new life, but the mom did not really earn the attention. Most babies are conceived by the parents having sex, conceiving, carrying a pregnancy for nine months and giving birth. It is not attention wrought from a four-year study in rocket surgery. It is a short-term event which is exciting and marvelous, but it is not usually the byproduct of a huge investment of time, resources and hard work.

The mother becomes attached to the attention surrounding pregnancy. She likes to be called Mommy before the baby is born. If Mother's Day comes around during the pregnancy she wants to be included. This is especially true if the mother is young; she has never experienced this level of attention from so many people in her life.

Most expectant mothers handle this attention well, some are annoyed by it and there are some who build their happiness upon it. When the blessed day arrives, the attention culminates into an effort to get the baby safely delivered. The two-day hospital stay is a whirlwind of close family and friends visiting and meeting the bundle of joy. Once the mother goes home, the attention drops dramatically. She may have some friends and family around to help with the newborn, but eventually the day comes when the mom is left alone with the baby and real family life begins. There are a few doctor appointments now and then, but most of the time she is on her own. The baby does not give attention and the mom transforms from the attention recipient to the attention giver.

If the mom is planning to return to work, she must find a childcare provider either before the baby is born or shortly thereafter. When the phone interviews begin, the mom gets a flashback of the attention she received as a pregnant mom. It feels great to have someone focus on YOU instead of the baby. The mom learns quickly that the potential childcare providers communicate with her in a way no one else has since she was pregnant. Goods or services she purchases for the baby are not complimented by a lot of face-to-face time with the service or goods provider. The childcare provider is different.

The moms who want to recapture the attention received as a pregnant mom will often become serial interviewers. They will spend days upon days contacting providers and arranging visits. They love sitting on the couches of the providers and talking about their birth experience and their newly found vast knowledge of their newborn. It is hard for them to pick a provider because once they do, the interview process is over. They often pick the provider who promises to acquiesce to their every whim; one who gives them the most attention during the interview and offers a care experience where her expertise as a parent is highly regarded. The provider may not be the cheapest or the most experienced, but she is the best at offering attention to the mother.

One of the interviewing challenges with the PASS mom is that she is interested in what she gets to do as opposed to what she must do. It is difficult to get her to focus on the policies and contract because she is more interested in what her role is in the child's care. She wants to come and have a peak time visit. She wants to be assured she can come early to watch how the baby does with the provider and stay after work to discuss the baby. In addition to onsite access, she wants the ability to call and text throughout the day. She is not interested in the rules such as paying on Friday for the upcoming week, illness policies, vacation and sick day policies or discipline methods. If she disengages while the provider is laying out the foundational business policies, they will become an issue immediately after the child begins care.

The first few days the parent will make numerous phone calls to check on the baby. The provider understands that a new parent is nervous and needs extra reassurance. They allow an unprecedented amount of contact to allay the fears of the mother as well as a wide breadth of time before and after daycare to answer any questions. They also receive evening and weekend texts as they teach the new mom the daycare ropes.

With the PASS mom, the level of contact she receives at the beginning of the relationship is expected even after the honeymoon period has passed. She continues to blow up the provider's phone many times a day and increases her arrival and departure visit time. She gets very upset if the provider does not answer the phone right away. She will put the provider on constant redial until the provider picks up. She will leave messages on the machine that begin with, "I know you must be busy" and escalate to, "Is there something wrong with MY baby? Why are not you answering?" I have counseled providers who have had mothers leave work and drive frantically to the childcare if they did not answer the phone or texts immediately. I have even heard a few stories of moms calling 911 for a welfare check.

As time goes on, the provider tries to lessen the time spent in communication with the parent. The provider can explain to the parent that she is busy and not to be worried if she does not answer right away. This is not acceptable to the PASS mom. She can assure the mom that no news is good news, but the mom is not satisfied.

When the mom asks questions about the child, she is angry if the provider states the child is doing fine. If the child is doing well in care, there is no fodder for conversation. The provider learns to be VERY selective about what concerns she DOES bring up because the storm of calls, texts and conferencing the parent will require to address the concerns far outweighs the benefit of any parental assistance.

When the provider is completely fed up with the constant intrusion she tells the mom she cannot answer the phone and do a conference every day as she has other kids and parents to manage. She explains to the mom that she has six kids and twelve parents and if she did twelve five-minute check-in calls every day, she would be working an hour a day just for check-in calls. The PASS mom tells her she does not want her to field the other parent's calls... just hers. The provider has to cut the mom off at some point because the money she is paying does not compensate for this level of conferencing.

The parent will try to create situations where the provider must interact with her for the best interest of the child. This parent uses phrases such as "does Pookie do XYZ at your house?" If the provider says no, the parent then engages the provider by describing at length what Pookie is doing at home. This concern somehow meanders its way into the care of the child. If the provider shares a concern about the child in childcare, the PASS parent says it does not happen at home so she needs to find out what is going on at the daycare that is causing the problem.

This attention seeking mom is very difficult to get in and out of the childcare during drop-offs and pick-ups. She thwarts every attempt the provider makes to get it down to a few minutes on each end. If the mom breastfeeds, she wants to breastfeed when she drops off the child and immediately when she picks up. This can lead to an unpaid hour a day of having the mom onsite while the provider is trying to work. The provider needs to evaluate whether this is necessary or just a way for the parent to force a captive audience. I would not choose a mother who needed an hour a day onsite to feed the baby. I expect the baby to be fed before the parent leaves from home and when they return home at the end of the day. If the feeding and pumping schedule is so tight that there is not another option the mother is willing to do, it will not work for my business.

If there is not an obvious reason for the parent to stay at drop-off and pick-ups, the PASS parent will create one. She will do whatever it takes to have a reason to stay in the childcare. If her child is not crying at drop-off, she will smother the child with kisses and goodbyes until she gets him worked up and crying. Then she has to stay to calm him down. She wants her child to be hysterical when she feigns leaving. She will say, "Mommy's leaving" and "Mommy loves you," repeatedly until the child goes ballistic. Once the child starts clinging to her she tries to engage him in some sort of play to distract him so she can leave. Once he calms down she starts the goodbye kisses and hugs again. I call this the "Mom Loves Baby Show." The credits roll when she FINALLY gets into her car to go to work. Before she puts the car in reverse, she quickly grabs her phone to post a Facebook status with a sad face and a lament of how her baby cried when she dropped him off at daycare and she wishes she did not have to work.

At pick-up, she will insist on staying even if the provider has the child completely ready to go. She will start plying the child with questions about where her toy or blanket is. She will claim the child is wet and needs to be changed. She will need a Kleenex to pick a booger out of the kid's nose. She will do ANYTHING to get her body into the play area so she can stay.

While she is hanging out at the provider's house she does not talk about the child. She complains about her job, her mother-in-law or her husband. She wants advice but does not listen to what is offered. She fixates on the other children and their parents. She engages the incoming parents and interjects into their conversations with the provider. In the meantime, her child is running rampant in the provider's house causing rack and ruin in areas he is never allowed to enter when the provider is caring for him.

She will seize ANY opportunity to go into areas of the house the provider has off-limits. She will open gates for her child to go into the family's private areas. She then chases after the child so she can have an excuse to go into those areas herself. She will get her child drinks out of the provider's refrigerator, food out of her cabinets and need to use the bathroom or kitchen sink to wash her hands.

If the provider is not on the exit level of the house and has to remain in a playroom to supervise the remaining children, the PASS parent will help herself to the entire upstairs. I have counseled providers who have had to confine all the children downstairs in order to go upstairs and demand the parent remove herself and her kid from her bedroom or her child's bedroom when they were sent home fifteen minutes beforehand. The parent feigns that it is beyond her control because Snowflake got loose.

If there is an upstairs play area the parent will allow her child to enter and destroy the room. It is a blast watching your child dump out a room. The kid loves doing it and the parent loves watching. She does not know, understand or care about the safety or cleaning measures the provider has in place in each area of the house. This parent can unknowingly put her own child and the other daycare children at risk by allowing cross-contamination of toys from one area to another. She does not care about the mess the provider has to fix.

I have heard far too many stories of these parents finally getting out the door and still remaining on the property. The provider will believe the family has left and realize forty-five minutes later that the mom and daycare kid are still on the front porch or outside on the provider's playground using the swingset, tricycles and cars.

Sometimes the provider's only way to get the parent to leave is to claim she has somewhere she has to go. Providers all over the country load their own kids in the car and drive around the block just to get the PASS parent to leave. It is an extreme measure, but it is the only way a provider knows how to get the parent to leave without risking the parent becoming upset and withdrawing the child from care.

This parent is one of the most difficult parents to have in a childcare business. To gain the attention and privilege they became accustomed to in their new status as "parent", they show a complete lack of boundaries and use their child and their money to prey upon a shy, weak or desperate provider who does not like conflict.

If the provider senses the interviewing parent is high maintenance, she needs to set boundaries for her time and her work at the very first interview. The first days the child is in care are crucial for setting limits on what this parent can have for the money she pays. Set a dollar amount for every minute after contracted time and, if possible, avoid allowing open to close hours for a flat fee.

Daycare Whispers...

Be cautious about how much interaction you allow this parent in the beginning. The parent will want more and more as time goes on.

When the parent is contacting the provider in an unnecessary fashion (evenings, weekends, many times throughout the day), pare down the responses to one or two word phrases. Gradually increase the time between when you receive the text or call and when you answer it.

When asked how the child is doing, answer "same" whenever possible.

When interviewing, make it clear that you do not host visits before or after daycare contracted hours.

If the parent remains in the childcare when she is supposed to be gone, be very blunt about not allowing it. Use phrases like, "It is time for you guys to scoot!"

The Lying Parent

Every business has to deal with dishonest customers. Childcare is no exception. Most consumer deceit is related to money; they want free or discounted goods or services.

There are several reasons parents mislead their childcare provider. As in most businesses, money lies are the most common, but there are several other deceptions that occur within the daycare world. Some parents use half-truths to promote their notion that their child is gifted, advanced or not delayed. They will lie to get the provider to provide services that make their life easier at home or to avoid having to care for their child on a daycare day. When managing parental lying, the conflict you have with the parent exponentially increases when you have two or more intentions rooted within a lie.

The top five categories of parental deception:

1. Health
2. Potty training
3. Late pick-up or early arrival
4. Payments
5. The child's behavior while under parental care

The Parent who Lies about Health

A new provider will experience health deception within the first month of doing childcare. Because it is by far the most difficult lie to vet, the parent will have had many times when they successfully sent an ill child to daycare and the provider was unaware. Every success minimizes the parent's confidence in the daycare provider's health policies and intensifies their belief that the provider's exclusion policies are unnecessarily strict.

Health deception is one of the common areas where the parent has multiple intentions for the deceit. A parent will lie about their child's health to protect their money and to ensure they do not have to care for their child during an illness. Their reasons may be so the parent can work or have free time without the child. The parent may use their paid time-off for kid-free days or their own illnesses. They often prefer to go to work rather than spend their day with a sick child.

Parental diagnosis of illness symptoms is almost always in this order:

1. teething
2. allergies
3. ear infection
4. tainted food
5. car sickness
6. blocked tear duct
7. cold in the eye
8. growing pains
9. intolerance to food group
10. fatigue

Notice anything about these diagnoses? Not one symptom is contagious. If the child is contagious, they are not allowed to attend childcare. In my 20 years of caring for kids, I have never had a parent come to me and say, "I think he has a contagious case of fill-in-the-blank." I think I would have to quit doing childcare if that phrase ever graced my ear buds. My faith in humanity would be restored and I would devote myself to world peace.

Parents will go to great lengths to cover up an illness. The most common method is the dope-and-drop. This is when a parent gives a fever-reducing medication such as Advil and Tylenol to mask the fever. Currently eight-hour Advil is used more frequently than Tylenol because it buys the parent almost the entire daycare day of the medication fooling the provider. When a short acting medication such as Tylenol is used, it can mask the fever until naptime. If the provider does not catch on to this deception, they will be unaware the child has a fever until after the child wakes up from their nap. This, at the least, buys a parent time to prepare for the inevitable twenty-four hour exclusion the following day.

Sometimes a parent will sense their child is sick and give them Tylenol or Advil as an insurance policy that the child will not spike a fever. There are also parents who medicate their children nearly every day for the same reason. These children receiving daily antipyretics can develop life-threatening illnesses such as kidney and liver failure. If you suspect this is happening, you are at serious risk of having a child die in your care. It is best to counsel the parent that this is very dangerous and that you cannot continue to care for the child.

If you have a child that comes at the same time day after day, week after week, year after year and one random day the parents call to say they are running late and will be there in an hour or so, be on alert. This could mean the parent is just waiting for the medication to kick in so they only miss part of their day. Always ask if the child woke up sick. A kid with a fever in the early morning could be a very sick kid by late afternoon. When the child arrives, ask the parent directly if the child has received any medication or woke up with any symptoms of illness. Watch the parent's response closely to detect any signs of deceit and watch the child closely for other signs of illness.

The Tylenol and Advil disguise is very hard to manage because it cannot be proven. I have had a number of instances where the child vomited their dose after arrival. When the parent was confronted, they insisted it was given for teething. This is why I have it in my policies that I do not provide service to children on Advil and Tylenol for any reason. If they have it on board, I cannot assess their body temperature. Fever is the number one indicator of health and if it is masked, I cannot be assured the child is not sick.

If the parent uncharacteristically comes for an early pick up on a day when the child appears "off" be suspicious. The parent may want to fetch the child before the medication wears off to safeguard having childcare the next day. You will not see this on a Friday or last day of care for the week. If the parent has the next day off there is not a need for an early pick up.

I do not give Advil or Tylenol for teething. I will not even do it with a doctor's order. I will give them pain medicine if a child has something severe like a broken bone or post-operative pain after a tonsillectomy. Other than these limited situations, I do not give fever reducing medications.

My friend, Stacey Jones, has an illness policy that is brilliant. She excludes children for two days if the child becomes ill at childcare. She excludes for one day if the parent keeps the child home voluntarily. This encourages parents to not attempt fever masking. However, it only works on the days where there are two daycare days left in the child's schedule.

There are some health issues that can cost a provider a serious amount of time and money without warning. These are head lice, bed bugs, scabies and fleas. The eradication of these pests can cost hundreds of hours of labor and many thousands of dollars. Bed bugs are extremely expensive to eradicate. I have known two providers who have lost their businesses over bed bugs. The parents knew they had bed bugs and knowingly brought the child to care without discussing it with the provider. The providers found out about the bugs because of bites on the child's arms and legs. The eradication required closing the business down and paying thousands of dollars in exterminator fees and product loss. One provider had an older home and the treatment to the home ruined the entire electrical system throughout the house.

A parent who knowingly sends their kids with bugs can rock your world. I make it a point to do a skin check on each kid every day during diaper changes. I check them from head to toe. If I notice anything that could remotely resemble a bite the parents are called. I also BEG the parent at the interview to let me know immediately if they have been exposed to any bugs. I give them my word that I have systems in place to still allow the child to attend. I will not think less of them and I will not punish them if they tell me upfront. I have helped families buy lice shampoo and spray, done laundry for them, provided daily free clean clothing, replaced toys and checked hair for the entire family. Catching bugs on the front end will save you both time and money and, quite possibly, even your business.

If I find out a parent knowingly sent a child with a pest infestation I will terminate them and sue for damages. I will devote my resources into punishing them. In my world there is absolutely no reason to deceive me. If they choose not to take my help when an infestation is first known, they will pay dearly by the time I am done with them.

I wish I could offer more solutions for dealing with health lying. If a parent deceives you by not disclosing medication, it is a lie by omission. You will deal with it regardless if you are a newbie or a veteran provider.

A common tell is if the parent uncharacteristically calls or texts to see how their child is doing. It may seem innocent enough, but often it is to gauge whether you have caught on. They are keeping their fingers crossed that you will not discover the illness so they do not have to come get the kid or miss work the next day.

The one thing I have learned is that when parents lie they do the exact same things as the ones who have lied before them. They believe they invented the lie and do not ever consider that you have been to this rodeo before.

With experience, you will find they say the same words. They use the same voice inflection, the same nonverbal behavior and the same gestures. They divert their gaze and use hedged words. Often with illness lying they attempt to use words to encourage you to provide extra supervision without fully admitting the extent of the child's symptoms. The phrases they use are: keep an eye on her, let me know if she does XYZ, she was a little off this morning, she's having a hard time with, she's extra tired today, etc. Learn those phrases and apply them to the outcomes you know. This way you will be educated the next time that parent uses the same words and the body language of deceit. You can build your detection skills for future occurrences with that parent and all the lying parents in your future.

Many providers choose to ignore parental health dishonesty. Even when discovering information that cannot be denied, the provider will look the other way. When you tell a parent you know for a fact they have intentionally misled you, they will often terminate the childcare. They are angry to have been caught and termination is the only way to remain in control and not have to deal with any consequences. A provider learns the first time they confront a parent and loses the kid that it is risky business to tell the parent you know they have lied. You have to decide for yourself if the illness deceit is worth losing the income.

Daycare Whispers…

Watch for the Advil and Tylenol disguise.

Have a blanket policy that children cannot attend on Advil or Tylenol for teething.

You will be confronted with illness lying with a few weeks or months of opening your childcare. You have to decide yourself if you will confront the parent as confrontation often leads to parents terminating care.

Assess the children's skin daily for signs of bug bites. Catching a pest infestation early can be the difference of thousands of dollars and many hours of labor.

The Parent who Lies about Potty Training

Potty training is a time in the provider-parent relationship that can end in termination if the parent is not satisfied. I have counseled over a hundred providers over the course of the last decade with serious issues with parents when the child did not potty train in the time frame the parents expected. A fair percentage of the unhappy parents switched child care in hopes of finding a provider who would allow their child to go into underwear based on the parental declaration that the child was completely trained at home.

Parents have many motivations to have their child potty trained. Some parents believe an infant, even one as young as nine months, can be trained. Even though the child does not speak, the parents believe a child's body language (elimination communication) will tell them when the child needs to go potty. If watched closely, the provider can get the child to the potty or sink in time for the blessed event. Childcare providers cannot ignore the other children while exclusively watching one child, waiting to pick up on their nonverbal cues. Along the same lines, it is impossible for a provider to hang an infant over a toilet or sink and just wait until the child goes potty.

The parents who want infant potty training become frustrated when they have success and the provider will not try their method. They try to educate the provider in their technique. At home, the parent has a high tolerance for accidents and missed opportunities. They have a tendency to overlook the accidents and only focus on the hits. They often exaggerate the child's abilities because they believe that any diaper saved is a victory. They will settle for saving one or two diapers in exchange for hours of work. At daycare, the cost of a couple of diapers, each less than a buck, compared to the cost of the worker to manage the intense one-on-one potty training will never align.

Most parents start discussing potty training when their toddler is around eighteen months old. A large number of parents attach giftedness to early potty training and want the bragging rights that inevitably come with an early trainer. This type of parent is much like the infant potty training parent in that they have a high tolerance for accidents. A diaper saved is fifty cents earned. Early potty training nets the parents a ton of attention and saves them a ton of money. Win-Win!

Parents hear stories from older generation relatives where they claimed to have had all the children trained by age of eighteen months. These grandparents and aunts fail to mention that before the 1970s it was common to use corporal punishment during toilet training. They definitely trained children at a younger age, but they used techniques we are unable to use today. Even with laws to protect children from mistreatment, more abuse occurs during potty training than any other developmental step.

They also listen to their age mate friends and family who brag about their gifted snowflake who trained young. I had a family who had a child in my care for eleven years. The girl came to me as a newborn. I remember exactly when the girl potty trained: I was out of state on vacation and received a phone call from the little girl to tell me she went all week without having an accident.

Years later the mom and I were talking and she mentioned another family friend who had a kid who was almost four and still was not trained. She could not understand this delay because her daughter trained right after she turned two. Her daughter's birthday was mid-summer and the vacation I took was at Christmas the year the child was three. The mom remembered her child training in the beginning of the second year when the truth was the child trained in the middle of the third year, just a few months younger than the family friend's child.

Now, I would not suggest this mom was lying about the age her daughter was trained. I think she just wanted to believe her child was early and advanced. She did not remember the numerous conversations we had about the child being uncooperative and how the only solution was for her to use the two week Christmas vacation to go full on and get her trained. We stay in touch and see each other frequently. It's a running joke for us to argue about when she was trained. Joke aside, the kid was three and a half!

With the desire for bragging rights of a gifted child and potential economical savings from not having to purchase diapers, parents will often put pressure on the provider to start the process by age two. Providers are usually open to putting a child on the potty during diaper changes if the child is cooperative. After all, the child is already undressed from the waist down so it is a natural time to try. This is time consuming for the provider if the child never goes potty.

The parents usually accept this initial attempt to potty train during diaper changes, but the tolerance wanes quickly. The day comes when they start insisting the child is doing well in their home and they want the child to come to daycare in underwear. Even after many conversations regarding childcare potty training policies, the parent may submarine the provider by showing up one day with the kid wearing underwear, carrying a sack of spare clothes and pronouncing him trained. If the provider does not have diapers onsite for the child, this can cause a showdown. This is the point where the parent is so invested they are willing to find a new daycare if the provider will not comply. The kids are usually old enough to talk and can answer the parent's questions about whether they wore a diaper during the day. It's not a situation where the provider can do as she wishes without the parent knowing.

Unfortunately, when potty training reaches this point, the provider often finds the child still unable to tell her in advance when they have to go potty. She ends up with damaged furniture, carpet, equipment and a serious amount of cleaning. The savings of a couple of dollars a day for a parent can turn into many hours and hundreds of dollars of expense to the provider. This is when the provider often finds out the parent is not being honest about the child's home training. When she is losing money and suffering damage throughout her home, the conversations get very specific because the provider wants to have the same success. After in depth discussions, the providers usually find the parent is using home techniques that are not workable in a daycare setting. These techniques include putting the child on the potty every half hour for twenty-five minutes at a time or allowing the child to run around completely naked at home. They may also use pull-ups at home, but do not want to have the expense of supplying them at daycare.

A child's success with these home techniques is NOT an indication he is ready to wear underwear at childcare. The parent believes that because the child spends the lion's share of their waking day in care, the provider will train them if forced. The enforcement comes when the parents only supply spare clothes and underwear.

I had an issue with the family of a four-year old whom I had taken care of since she was 18-months old. The mom came to my daycare wanting the child to begin training. I explained that I do not attempt to train until the child is verbal enough to say the words "I have to go potty." She accepted this and did not mention it for another year. The kid's very limited verbal skills and developmental delays became more pronounced as she aged.

The mom was very resistant to discussing the child's obvious special needs as she was fixating on potty training as proof the child was normal. She began initiating daily conversations about how well the child was doing with potty training at home. She would even call me from Wal-Mart to announce the kid was in underwear and had asked to use their potty. The child had never uttered a phrase like that in my home.

The mom dropped off and the dad picked up. The dad was a talker and he told me the stories of all the potty accidents at home. The parents fought about it because he worked hard to provide a nice home and furnishings, but the mom's insistence the kid wear underwear was causing a great deal of damage to their house.

I did not tell Mom that Dad was telling me completely opposite stories. I knew the mom was exaggerating the child's potty training abilities. Since I needed the income, I simply kept the kid in diapers the entire time she was in my house. Even though I stopped conferencing about it with the mom at drop-off, every morning she would stand at my door and try to get her child to say the words "I have to go potty." The girl simply could not say it. When the time was drawing near for her to begin preschool, the mom found out being potty trained was a requirement. The pressure was really on now because the parents had paid upfront a half-year of tuition and they did not want to lose the slot.

Their emergency was not my problem. The child was still not potty trained despite my daily attempts to give her plenty of opportunities. My agreement with the parents was that she would wear diapers at my house, but I would put her in underwear right before she went home each day. One day just two-weeks before preschool was to begin, the mom was highly upset and insisted she come to daycare in underwear. Declaring it had been many months since she had an accident at their house, she blamed me for confusing her child. That same day, the dad came to pick up and asked me to diaper the child for the ride home. When asked why he wanted her in a diaper, he told me she had flooded his car seat the night before and he was tired of removing and cleaning the car seat cover. We only lived a mile apart and the child could not even make it home without an accident. He also told me that same night the child was sitting on his lap and she peed on both him and the recliner.

The mom knew about both of these incidences and still came the next morning demanding underwear on the child and proclaiming she had been accident-free for months. With the child leaving in less than two weeks and the parents having paid their final payment, I felt it was time to let the mom know I knew she had been lying all along. I told her the dad told me she was not accident-free at home and that she had just peed in the car seat and on the dad in the chair two days ago. Realizing I knew the truth all along, the mom was furious; she left with the kid and never came back.

I learned a lot from that family. I had many occurrences of this type of lying and developed very strict and measurable guidelines for managing potty training in my home. As long as the parents agree to supply the diapers so my home and time are protected, I do not care about their success (or lack thereof) at home. I learned with this family to set limits on how much I would conference about it because the parent's mission was to have her kid in underwear here. Every conversation came down to will I or will I not allow it. The answer was no every day. I had a bigger problem with the time lost at the front door than of the lying. I knew if I confronted the mom about the lying I would lose the kid, so I stayed out of it until I received the last payment we agreed upon. As I predicted, she left the day she was confronted about her lies.

I learned another lying lesson. When you want the truth, try Dad. It does not always work, but the dad often does not know enough about the mom's reasons for the deception. This happens with all daycare business conflict, not just potty training. The dads do not normally read the contracts and policies well enough to know what is or is not allowed. That's often left to mom. The only challenge is in knowing when to show your hand to mom when she is less than truthful. The first time you call her out, one of two things will happen: either the child will be pulled out of daycare or the dad will get schooled to keep his mouth shut. There will only be one time you'll get away with letting Mom know that Dad told a different story; so be judicious when spilling the beans if you cannot afford to lose your income – or your unwitting informer.

One last note about potty training lies – there is a way to recognize when you are being told the truth. Occasionally you'll have a parent tell you they are going full barrel at home, but you do not see the same indicators. One thing these truth tellers have in common is they preface their bragging with "I know you might not be able to do this with Johnny here, but I have been doing XYZ at home and he is doing well." They will make it clear that if you want to try it, they would be happy, but they do not expect you to do it. They are happy they are saving diapers and moving the child toward successful home training. When the parent understands you have a different life with a house full of kids and different sanitation requirements and does not insist you copy their ways or have the same good outcome they have, they are telling the truth.

When the pressure is off and you can decide for yourself how to proceed, sometimes you end up with a young one who surprises you and potties like a rock star at both home and daycare.

Daycare Whispers...

Potty training is second only to illness as the most common form of parental lying.

Even with laws to protect children from abuse, more harm occurs during potty training than any other developmental step.

Insist a child be able to say the words "I have to go potty" before you will even consider training.

It is common for parents to terminate the childcare arrangement if a provider refuses to allow untrained children to come to childcare in underwear.

Often the parent is using home training techniques a provider is not willing or legally able to use.

If you want the truth of the child's potty training success, ask Dad. Once you bring up the dad's story to Mom, the dad will stop talking.

Be able to tell when a parent is telling the truth about potty training success at home. This is when they do not demand your participation, but are truly grateful for your assistance.

The Parent who Lies about Late Payment

Parents can come up with some pretty spectacular reasons not to pay their child's tuition on time. If the provider allows payments at the end of service rather than before the service is provided, they will run the risk of having parents delay payment. The parent has already gotten what they wanted, so they can withhold payment until they need service again.

Providers depend on their salary to pay for their home and business expenses. They can fret away their free time after work waiting for parents to show up with a payment. If the parent does not pay until after the banks are closed, access to the credit is delayed further.

One of the techniques parents use to excuse their late payment is to add layers to how and when they will get the money they need to pay the provider. They will claim their paycheck is late, their bank is closed, their mom needs to go cash their check, the bank misplaced their deposit, someone bounced a check to them so their account is in arrears, etc. The more layered the excuse becomes, the less likely the provider is to receive the money and the more likely the parent is going to ask for the child to continue coming without the payment. Listen to what they are saying and write down how many things need to go right for you to get the money. If there are two or more hurdles to overcome to get the money to you, you will not be getting it.

Once they place something between their money and the provider that is beyond their control, they will have placed a marker on the payment. They have only to answer as to what is happening with the delay instead of what they owe the provider.

A bounced check is a late payment and a parental fraud. If parents knowingly pay a provider with a bad check to buy time, they lied the second they placed the check in the provider's hand. Whatever excuse they come up with is unacceptable. They need to have the money on hand at all times. Do not allow online bill pay checks cut at a bank to be sent to you for the weekly tuition. Once the parent states the check was ordered and the money has been withdrawn from their account, it could take weeks before an error in processing is righted (if the parent even ordered the check in the first place). If something has happened to their money, they need to borrow the money from someone other than their daycare provider.

Withholding payment is borrowing money.

When interviewing, the provider MUST take a tough, unwavering stance on late payments. A painful daily fee for late payment and a two-strikes-you-are-termed rule dissuades nearly all parents from considering being late.

The biggest deception in late payments occurs when a parent KNOWINGLY brings their children to care when they do not or will not have the funds to cover the fee. They carry on as if nothing is wrong and do not apprise the provider of the problem until the time comes to pay. They often send someone else to pick up the children so they do not have to face the provider. They sometimes will keep the children home the last day of the payment cycle in order to avoid the confrontation. When the parents owe money and refuse to answer phone calls and texts, the provider knows she has been intentionally deceived. The provider should never have to chase down her money.

The only way to avoid the late payment lying is to set very strict standards and always impose the fees to which they agreed. Unless the parent or child is in intensive care on life support or the bank burned down to the ground, the payment should be on time. A sick kid does not a good late payment excuse make. The parent needs to get the money to the provider no matter what is going on.

Childcare should be the very first bill a parent pays. Do not let their words convince you otherwise and NEVER receive the child until the fees are paid up.

NO pay = NO stay.

Daycare Whispers…

Watch for parents using multiple layered excuses as to why they cannot pay on time. The more obstacles to them getting money and giving it to you, the higher likelihood they do not have the money at all.

Do not allow parents to borrow money from you by way of free services.

Be clear with parents at the interview that payment for childcare needs to be the first bill they pay.

A post-dated check is a late payment.

A bounced check is a lie.

Have a very steep late payment fee and do not forgive it a single time.

The Parent who Lies about Early Arrival and Late Pick Up

One of the more difficult lies to manage in childcare is the deception surrounding the reason parents arrive early for drop-off or late for pick up. Refusal to adhere to the contracted service times causes conflict in the relationship and leaves the provider feeling used without compensation. If the consequence is not drastic, the behavior continues. If severe penalties are imposed, the clients leave.

The excuses for being early or late are often untrue. They usually boil down to something beyond the parent's control. A parent believes if they can convince the provider they were a victim and not at fault, then they can get out of the late fees and the provider will not be angry. With experience, the provider can circumvent many of the common tactics used by the parents to be early or late without fines or penalties.

In twenty years of service and four years of counseling providers on this issue, I believe I may have heard it all. The parents come up with some pretty fantastical excuses and I am always impressed when they conjure up one I have not heard yet. I love the creativity but do not enjoy having the kid outside the daycare clock.

The most common excuses for being late when picking up are:

- Stuck in traffic
- Boss kept me after work
- Long line at the bank
- Car would not start
- Had to go get gas
- Fell asleep at home and the alarm did not go off
- My phone died and the alarm did not go off
- My phone died and I did not know what time it was
- Someone else was supposed to pick up and forgot

- Roads were slick
- Doctor or dentist running late
- Road construction road backed up
- Flat tire
- Forgot my kids (yes, you read that right)
- Got pulled over for a speeding ticket
- Stuck by a train
- Lost my keys
- Forgot to put the car seat in the car

Annoying reasons for being late:

- "I had to go to the bank to get YOUR pay. Do you want paid or not?"
- "I had to stop to get gas. I cannot leave Snowflake in the car when I go into pay and he acts up in the Quickie Mart."
- "I had to stop to get gas or I would not have been able to make it to your house."
- "I had to go home and get dinner started because Pookie will not let me cook when we get home."
- "I had to go pick up my checkbook or paycheck."
- "I had to stop by the grocery store to get (insert sale item). I did not want to drag the kids with me because they act up at the store."
- "I had to stop by charity shop to get some free (insert food, clothes, diapers) and I got some for you."
- "I needed some time alone so I went walking. My old babysitter would have wanted me to have some time to myself because it makes me a better mother."
- "I was waiting in line to get the new iPhone."

Spectacular reasons for being late:

- "I got arrested so my mom has to pick up the kids."

- "I have a condition where I cannot do number two at work. I had to run home to do my business and it took a long time."
- "My granny died (again)."
- "I fainted after my vasectomy and woke up late."
- "There was a skunk in my driveway and I could not pull out."

The all-time ultimate grand supreme winner:

- "My wife and I were trying to conceive number two and it took longer than I thought."

Of the common and annoying reasons for being late, the newbie parents think they invented them. Like with most parental deception, they believe they are the first parent slick enough to come up with the excuses. What they do not realize is that not only has the provider heard every one of them before, but she can tell they are lying by the look on their face and the tone and inflection of their voice.

There are certain situations that increase the likelihood of a parent being late. One of the biggest predictors of a parent being late is when they tell you they are coming early. I always tell them to text me when they are nearby and not to bother calling me until then. I also am VERY firm that they cannot be later than the normal pick up time.

The only exception for a parent not being late (when they say they will be early) is when a child has a doctor appointment or the parent is traveling out of town. If the parents are driving out of town and want the child to sleep during the trip they will usually come during nap and pick up. However, if you volunteer to keep the child up until they arrive, they will not come early. NEVER keep a kid up based on a parent coming to get them during nap - not even five minutes. If they are running late because they are packing, they would prefer the child be awake at your house rather than at home with them while they finish getting ready. They just want to make sure the kid will fall asleep in the car.

If a parent has a grandparent from out of town visiting and they are running around together, they will change their mind about picking up early once they are out and about. They will come up with stories about why plans have changed. The whole process of them going from "I am going to pick up early" to "something happened TO me so I cannot" means a ton of calls as they change their minds and postpone it a half an hour at a time. I do not want to field the constant change of plans, so one heads up call when they are five minutes out is all I need.

My normal response when they say they are coming early is to tell them to just make the five-minute heads up call and then the whole thing goes POOF out of my brain. I do not give it a single thought. If they come early, that is great. If they do not come early, it is what I expected. No harm, no foul. This technique saves them from having to come up with stories to justify them not showing up when they said they would.

Another common situation where parents are late and intentionally deceive the provider is in inclement weather. If a parent is released from work early to avoid bad roads in traffic they will use it as an opportunity for running errands and getting supplies before they pick up the kid. They get caught up in the stores with all the other people who are also trying to stock up. This can cause them to be very late, but they do not worry about it because most providers allow parents to be late if the roads are really bad.

If the roads are bad, the parents are extremely late and their children are the last ones out the door, I go out to the car with the kids and check the front and back seat of the car. If all of the other kids were picked up reasonably close to when they are normally picked up and one family is unrealistically late, there is a good chance the parent went shopping. If I see groceries in the car, I call them out on it. That is when they give me the excuse they picked them up on their lunch break.

Confronting them the first time does not stop them from trying it again. They just put the groceries in the trunk the next time. It is a good idea to go out to the car with the kids on every really late pick up. It lets the parent know you will check the car both inside and out.

If they give you a flat tire excuse check the tires. If they get by with a flat tire excuse one time, they will try it again. Get a good look at their tires so you know what they look like for the next time they try it. They may have a donut or an odd tire on the car if they had a flat. If not, just seeing you look at their tires may give them pause the next time they try this excuse.

My policy for being late is simple: Don't do it.

I do not impose late pick up fees; I simply terminate. I tell them at the interview that I do not tolerate late pick-ups. Unlike some providers, I do not have a dollar per minute late fee because I do not want the money. I want them to pick up on time. When they are late any more than five minutes I say the same thing each time "You are REALLY late." I set the bar at the five-minute mark and I let them know I consider anything over five minutes as REALLY late. I do not want them to have the opportunity to say words like "it is ONLY twenty minutes late" or "I was just a little late" when they are a half hour late. Five minutes is REALLY late. Five minutes at the end of my day is a long time to me.

The other thing I do to avoid being put in the position of vetting their lies about being late is to build into each contract an additional ten minutes every day for the travel to and from work. I base my rates on departure time so they pay for that ten minutes every day. If something happens to them on the way home, they have ten minutes to figure it out or they will be late. If all goes well, they pick up ten minutes before they have to.

I do not take clients who tell me they could be late because sometimes they have to stay at work or stay on a call while at work. If you agree to even one allowance for them to be late they will use it every time.

I am very firm with work from home parents who live nearby. If the trip is short, they do not think it is a big deal if they leave their house when they are supposed to be at my house. I do not tolerate lateness even if it is no big deal to the parent. If they want open hours to come and go as they please, they need to find someone else.

The average parent will have something happen to them twice a year. In cold weather states, you will have delayed pick-ups with blizzards and ice storms. If they are late more than two times a year for non-weather situations or if they start being late right after they enroll, you have a parent who does not respect the pick-up time.

A parent who is mistakenly late or has a solid reason to be late will bring you money right away and apologize profusely. If they are solid clients and respect my business, I do not make a big deal of it. If I start hearing lies, stories and excuses on a consistent basis, I ask them to leave or extend their contracted pick up time later in order to allow more travel time. They have to pay for that every day whether they need it or not. Since this increases their weekly rate most parents do not take me up on the offer.

A modern late parent issue that has cropped up now that most people have cell phones is where the parent arrives on time, but sits in the driveway talking on the phone instead of coming in the house to get the child. The parent uses the excuse that they are talking to their boss or client during that time so they cannot help it. I have taken kids from the front door to the driver's side door many times to force them to take their kid. They are not on time if they are on the property but do not take possession of the child. I do not let them bully me by pretending it is okay to force me to keep the kid while they "work."

This phone issue does not happen at drop-off. The parent who is on the phone during drop-off is able to manage to get the kids from the car to my front door quite easily. That same parent can get the kids from my front door to the car just as easily. It is easier for the parent to have the provider watch the kids while they are on the phone. It is easier for the parent to do everything without their kids. If our work is based on what is easiest for the parent, they would never go home.

Arriving Early

I have more issues with parents trying to drop-off early than arrive late. I try to avoid this by saying exactly that in the first interview. Parents believe that it is no big deal to have their kid early if they have something to do in the morning that is easier without their child. Again, it is ALWAYS easier to do EVERYTHING without a child.

I have had parents arrive a half-hour early without asking if they could drop-off early. I tell them I cannot manage it and to come back at the time they are scheduled. I will not even do five minutes early unless the roads are bad. If you allow five minutes, it will escalate to ten within a few days; ten turns into fifteen, fifteen into twenty and twenty into a half hour within a few weeks.

The timeframe a parent will try to dump their kids off early is unpredictable. If their kid gets up early, the parent wants to get them buckled in the car and off to your house. They will sit in the driveway with their kid buckled in for as long as you will allow rather than have them up and running at home. I do not allow parents to sit in the driveway waiting for me to open my doors or until it is time for them to drop-off. If they want to sit in a car with their child they can sit out on the street.

When parents try to ambush a provider with their early arriving kids they will try to convince the provider that they HAVE to do this or that before work or go in early. If they do not ask the provider permission, it is a clear sign they are lying. If they truly have something they must do, they will call and make arrangements BEFORE they agree to do it. But when they really have to get gas, coffee or meet up with a friend before work, they will lie and say it has something to do with their job. The underlying threat is that if they do not keep their job, you will not be able to take care of their kid.

The best way to avoid the early drop-off lies is to tell them at the first meeting how parents before them have tried to force you into taking the kids early and you do not allow it. Set boundaries so that they know all the fantastic stories they can come up with will not work. If they are asked to go into work early, they need to ask permission for you to take the kids. They cannot assume they will force you into it by arriving early and banging your door down or letting their kid rapid-fire ring the doorbell.

Attach a steep fee for an early drop-off. I do a dollar per minute by appointment and I do not take the child at all if previous arrangements have not been made. Once they know I will not be a part of the cycle, they do not put energy into trying to deceive me into allowing it.

Daycare Whispers…

Parents believe they invented the common lies.

One of the biggest indications a parent is going to be late is when they tell you they are coming early.

NEVER keep a kid up at nap based on a parent's words that they are coming early to pick them up.

Parents use their early release from work on inclement weather days to run errands and have time for themselves.

Anything over five minutes is REALLY late. Tell the parent this the first time they go beyond five minutes.

Best policy for late pick-ups is "Do not do it."

The closer the parent is to your home, the earlier they will arrive and the later they will pick up. You will have more issues with parents picking up late when they work close by than parents who work far away.

Do not allow parents to talk on their cell phones in your driveway.

The Parent who Lies about Home Behavior, Care and History

Children often behave very differently in childcare than they do at home. This is a given in nearly all provider-parent relationships. The closer you are in beliefs and childcare methods, the less likely you are going to have problems bleed over from home into daycare. The wider the gap in philosophies, the more pronounced and frequent the differences will arise. It is within these differences where parents can manipulate the truth of their care and behavior of the children and present a picture that does not mesh with what you are seeing with the child in your home.

Sleep Lying

Sleep lies are the most dangerous of all lies as they can lead to infant death.

Early in the relationship parents learn the sleep methods a provider can legally use. Some providers do not follow safe sleep practices and allow the parents to give permission verbally or in writing to adhere to the parent's sleep preferences. These include allowing babies to sleep in swings, beds, car seats, couches, floors, etc. They also use blankets and lovies. Some providers believe if the parent agrees to their baby sleeping in infant equipment or anywhere other than a crib or playpen, they can allow it. They may also allow babies to sleep on their tummy per the parent's request. Providers who follow State laws, regulations and best practice do not allow sleeping in anything other than an empty crib or playpen with only a tightly fitted mattress sheet. They do not allow any cloth in the crib and put the baby to sleep on their back.

It is becoming increasingly rare to find parents who practice safe sleep despite the availability of safe sleep information on the internet and training from the providers who are following their State laws. Some parents believe that crying causes brain trauma because of research done on Romanian orphans with brain damage. Dr. Richard Sears, the leading expert on attachment parenting, uses some of this research and applies it to normally parented babies. He then sells his method of parenting with this research being the foundational rationale for interceding and stopping the crying. The new parent who has been deceived by these mishandled research results believes that if their baby cries, the baby's cortisol levels rise, causing damage to their brain.

The effort to stop all crying leads parents to use comfort and sleep methods that are dangerous. Co-sleeping in the same bed, sleeping in a car seat outside of the car, bouncer seats and swing sleeping are very dangerous. Breastfed infants sleeping all night surrounded by blankets, attached and suckling their mother's nipple is becoming increasingly common. Providers are not allowed to use these methods while the child is in care. They are unable to mimic the side laying suckling at the mother's breast when the baby goes to sleep.

Because of this, nearly every infant entering childcare has a terrible time adjusting. They may have never had a single day, since being in the nursery at the hospital, where they have slept alone, face-up on a flat surface crib or playpen. When the provider discusses and educates the parent about the sleep practices and comfort measures she can use, the parent is often put on notice that if they continue to use the methods they have used at home, the baby will cry and will not adjust easily to the daycare protocol.

Many parents will continue to have their babies sleep in unsafe sleeping positions even when they know the baby may die. They do not want the brain damage and they do not want to listen to the crying. They think like teenagers: it happens to other people, not them. I have worked with a family whose lives were decimated after they lost their first born to positional asphyxia. It was devastating to watch the grieving and the daily, unrelenting pain this family endured. I also have two close friends who lost their first grandchild to co-sleeping deaths. Until we start charging and prosecuting parents for baby deaths as we do providers, mainstream society parents will be willing to take the risk.

The parent may try to convince the provider that with their rights as a parent, they should be able to give permission for the provider to use these methods too. They cannot. Parents can't give permission to do the wrong thing.

When the provider realizes the baby is not going to accept sleeping on its back, the parent is often given an ultimatum to either get the baby used to safe sleeping or find another daycare. The parent who needs childcare tomorrow claims they will work on it. Three days of back sleeping on a hard surface alone is what it takes for the average baby to adjust. When the parents have the child home from Friday evening until Monday morning the baby should make a huge amount of progress.

The parents often claim they are requiring the baby to sleep this way, but most do not. If the parent is willing to continue the ruse of saying they are having the baby back sleep on a flat surface when they actually are not, they are risking the life of the baby. A provider can tell whether or not the baby has been sleeping on their back despite the parents words. Without asking, an experienced provider can tell exactly what the parent is doing by the way a baby presents.

The majority of intentional injury and death of infants in childcare is rooted in the provider not being able to cope with crying. She may dope the baby with Benadryl or shake the baby in anger. She may use unsafe sleeping measures to stop the crying. It does not matter if the provider is new, in the middle of her career or a twenty-year veteran. Reacting to crying in a deadly way knows no age or years of experience. Of course, most providers will not go to such extremes, but some will. It is not worth the risk.

In May of 2014 a veteran childcare provider in South Dakota, Cindy Jo Hanisch, had a three-month old newborn baby die in her care. She put the baby to bed swaddled in a blanket face down. When asked why she used this unsafe position to sleep the baby her answer was "the parents asked me to not allow him to cry too long and children fall asleep easier on their stomachs."

One of the best insurance policies parents can put in place to protect their baby when in the care of another person (childcare or otherwise) is to manage sleep and crying without unsafe or unrealistic practices. The parent who lies about what they are doing at home to manage sleep is very dangerous to a childcare provider and to the baby. If the baby can only sleep in unsafe positions, the parent needs to keep them home and take the risk alone.

Another common sleep lie is about how much the child sleeps at home. When a parent starts complaining the child is awake late into the night, it is important to ask what time they went to bed. I have had parents complain about their child waking up in the middle of the night and when I ask what time they go to bed, I am told a couple of hours after they picked the child up from daycare. If the kid is picked up at five and is in bed by seven, they do not have any family awake time other than traveling home, supper and baths.

Kids need to play at home and go outside with their parents when the weather permits. A trip to the park or a bike ride can make all the difference. They need a full home life and this cannot be achieved in only two hours a day with their parents. They need quantity time not quality time. You cannot have quality time if you do not have quantity time. I encourage the parent to keep the child up until nine. This will resolve the issue of waking up during the night. They can go outside on a bike ride or trip to the park. They can have playtime together and do arts and crafts. Any family activity that is active, not passive, fulfills the children so they do not need to get up or stay up late into the night.

Health Lying

In addition to parents lying about their child's health by bringing them to daycare when they are sick, there are other areas related to health that often come up. These do not prevent the child from attending daycare, but do affect what is done when they are in care.

I had a terrible experience five years ago with a new client who had a baby boy. She was a doctor and was referred to me by one of my favorite families. I normally do not take friends of friends because if one becomes unhappy or leaves for any reason, you can easily lose both kids. If they decide they want a policy change they can come to the provider as a team and expect change because they are such a high percentage of the business income. It was risky, but I decided to take the chance because the money and hours were great.

The baby came on a Friday a week before he was to start full time. He had been in free grandma care before coming, so I knew it was going to be a long hard day. Surprisingly the little bundle of cuteness did really well.

The mom called me the next day (not a good sign for a new client to bother me on the weekend) and was hysterical. She told me her son was really sick and had a rash all over his body. He had horrible mouth ulcers and was screaming in pain. She demanded to know what I exposed him to and if any of the other children were sick with a high fever and a rash. I told her that none of the children had been sick for well over a month and they were all present and accounted for the previous day. They did not have a rash, fever, mouth ulcers. Nothing.

She told me she would have to rethink daycare because her child only came for one day and he was already sicker than he had ever been in his life. She implied the child was sick from something I did. I knew it was impossible because I do not allow new babies to have access to any of the other kids until they have been with me for at least a week. We do one-to-one care for the first week. I knew it could not be true, but she did not.

I did not hear back from the mom for the rest of the week. On the Friday before he was supposed to officially start daycare she called and said she would bring over the paperwork for the daycare and pay me for the upcoming week. She brought his physical and shot record. She had the physical form completed by his pediatrician the day he was sick with the high fever and rash. After she left, I looked over the immunization form and the physical. Low and behold, the physical form had a diagnosis of herpangina. This is a coxsackie virus with a three to ten day incubation period. There was no chance the child had picked it up at my house because the minimum incubation period is three days and the kid broke out in the rash and blisters less than twenty-four hours after leaving my house.

The mom was a doctor and knew once she received the diagnosis that she had accused me of something I could not have possibly done. She never apologized. She also knew that her child was in my home with a house full of kids, including her best friend's child, but she did not have the decency to tell me the truth so that I could warn all of my other clients that their child had been exposed to this painful and scary illness. She did not know I hadn't allowed her child to be around the other kids that day.

She lied by omission because not only did she not want to admit that she was wrong, but HER child had brought illness into the daycare. She demanded to know if another child exposed her, but did not give a flip about telling me what I needed to know to warn the other parents of what her kid exposed them to.

Lying by omission is still lying. This parent would have been terminated immediately if she hadn't been a friend of one of my all-time favorite families. This incidence was the first of a series of occurrences with her that led me to honor her with the second of only two terminations related to parental behavior I had to do in twenty years of operating a daycare. Lie to me once and I will give you one more chance. Lie to me again and you are gone.

I have also had parents who were upset with a health exclusion and denied the most likely diagnosis I offered. I had a kid with ringworm whose mother insisted was eczema. She tried to hide the spot with a bandage for a few days. Once the bandage fell off, it was obvious it was not a single round patch of eczema. Ringworm is contagious. Eczema is not. The mother was upset at the exclusion, but she took the child to the doctor and got a return to daycare note for two days later. The doctor's note did not contain a diagnosis. I needed the diagnosis so I could inform my other clients of the exposure. She refused to admit she was wrong and kept the diagnosis out of the paperwork. She claimed it was an unknown rash, but the medication prescribed was for ringworm.

This was a save face lie. The parent could not admit that the foot stomping and anger she had for being forced to take her child to the doctor turned out to actually be for a contagious disease. She did not want to admit she had behaved badly so she REFUSED to admit my concern was founded.

Injury Lying

One of the biggest fears all providers have is that a parent will bring a child to daycare after the child was injured or harmed intentionally and not tell the provider. I have had kids who fell down a flight of stairs when they were with the parents and they did not say a single word to me at drop-off.

If the parent thinks they will be in trouble for an injury that happens to their child, they may not seek medical treatment. They are more likely to take a wait-and-see approach before admitting they were not properly supervising the child. If the child is in my house and I do not know about the injury the see part of the wait-and-see does not happen. This puts the child and my business at risk.

If a parent does a midday check in on the child when they typically never call during the day, be suspicious. If a parent tells you to keep an extra eye on the child for whatever reason, find out EXACTLY what happened to cause the parent to bring this up. They may minimize it because they do not want to take the child to the doctor and they do not want to miss work. A concussion can take days to show up if it is a slow bleed. The parent may think the child is out of the woods when they really are not.

A friend of mine had a child brought to her after falling off a changing table. The parents did not say a word. When the provider noticed the child was lying around and favoring one side, she called the parents to find out if something had happened. Of course, she feared she would be blamed. The child was picked up, taken to the hospital and discovered to have had a broken leg.

It is critical to check every kid from head to toe when they arrive. Never allow a parent to bring in a sleeping child. Never allow a baby to remain sleeping in a car seat. Get the baby out and awake. You cannot tell level of consciousness on a sleeping kid. You cannot tell if they are normally mobile if they are confined or asleep.

Medication Lying

Medication lying can be frustrating to deal with - especially regarding nebulizer treatments. Neb treatments are very time consuming and parents often want most or all treatments to be done at childcare. If the child needs an every four-hour treatment when they get up in the morning, the parent may drop the child off to care and tell the provider the child had one at four a.m. It would be too early for the parent to give the treatment at home but due right when the child arrives at childcare. If the medication is every four hours and the child is in care nine hours, the provider must do three treatments on her clock. This can easily take a full hour of one-to-one care.

I quit offering nebulizer treatments because of parents abusing the privilege of having them done during care. I passed bags of medication back and forth with the parents and counted the number of medication jets in the bag. I had many instances of the child returning with the same number of jets they had when they left my house the day before. It was clear the parents were not only lying about giving treatments in the middle of the night to avoid giving them right before daycare, but that they were not giving them at all. They figured three per day was enough (or good enough) as long as I administered all three. The day my staff assistant and I did twenty treatments in one day was the day I was done. If the child needed daytime treatments they had to stay home with the parents until they did not.

I only offer medication if it is prescribed four times a day or more. If it is three or fewer times per day, the parents give all the doses at home. This stops parents from dumping all the doses onto the daycare. I do not give over-the-counter medication and do not allow children to attend when on over-the-counter medications.

Often parents do not want to fight the child when giving eye drops or yucky tasting medications so they try to involve the daycare provider in the doses. It is not unusual to find out that the parent did not do any on their clock. The parents seem to do better if they have all the responsibility rather than some.

Some parents try so hard to get out of doing the medications that they will call the doctor and get a medication time order that puts all of the doses on the daycare clock. They lie to the doctor and say the child will not take it when they first get up or some other excuse of why it has to be done at daycare. I handle this by calling the doctor and telling them the parent can do it before daycare, after daycare and at bedtime. I will not be forced into giving medication when the parents can manage it completely without involving me.

Feeding Lying

A common feeding lie we are seeing in childcare is that a breastfed baby can drink out of a bottle when they cannot. This discussion comes up on daycare.com and other childcare boards often. An unsuspecting provider believes the mother when she says her child takes a bottle.

The mothers who breast feed and have to return to work have an obligation to prepare the baby to eat when she will be away from the baby. If the mother does not devote herself to this concept and practice bottle feeding daily before the baby goes into care, the baby will not be able to eat away from the mom.

The mother may not be able to feed the bottle to the baby because the baby will refuse when having access to the breast. The mother may have to have the father, relatives or friends give the bottle. It does not matter to the provider WHO bottle feeds the baby, she just wants to know for sure the baby has learned how to eat from it.

If the baby cries and refuses the bottle, the moms will not hold off feeding until they willingly take it. The mom cannot bear to listen to the crying and she does not want to do the work of pumping when she has the baby wanting to eat. Some moms have magical thinking that the baby will just get hungry enough to take the bottle even though she refuses every attempt at home. This mom will tell the provider the baby takes some milk by bottle and they are working on it. Those are the key phrases that should alert the provider that the baby does not do it at all.

The older the baby, the harder it is to get them to convert to a bottle nipple. If the mom does not require that the baby take at least a bottle a day before the baby starts daycare, the baby will most likely not be able to manage a bottle. Training the baby almost always means the baby will cry and have to have feedings withheld for the baby to get hungry enough to take the nipple. The mom does not want the baby to cry.

Some mothers believe it is the childcare provider's job to get the baby on the bottle. There is little in daycare that takes a provider to the seventh level of hell as quickly and as intensely as a brand new baby shrieking from hunger pains, unable to take breast milk from a bottle. It is horrible. The mom may expect the provider to do the grueling feeding a few sucks at a time or even squirt it in by syringe. This does NOT work because the baby spits it out while crying and burns off more calories screaming than can be consumed from those few milliliters of breast milk. The provider has to completely devote every minute of the day to a baby who can only take in a couple of teaspoons at a time. It is difficult enough integrating a newborn into a group of kids; putting this burden on the provider is asking way too much.

The mother may tell the provider it is okay for the baby to go all day without eating because she cluster feeds all night. The mother may want to come and feed the baby at drop-off, on her lunch break and at pick-up. I do not accept this because I do not host breastfeeding and I do not want a baby in my house that cannot eat. My rule is every child in the house must be able to eat. No exceptions.

There is one way to avoid this lying parent. Require the baby to come to your house within two days of the first day of care and eat a bottle in front of you. NO exceptions. The baby must be able to woof, chow, hork down, gobble, slam a baby bottle before they can come to my house. I do not provide the service of bottle training and I do not recommend any other provider become involved in it either.

Another common food lie is that the child eats a healthy diet when, in fact, they live off of junk food and treats. The best plan for kids over the age of one is to do a food intake questionnaire that asks SPECIFIC food questions. I ask what non-fried, non-breaded meat, green vegetables and uncooked fruits they eat. That is all you really need to know because the common foods in a picky kid's diet do not include plain meat, green vegetables and fresh, whole fruit.

The parent of the picky eater wants to make it seem like the kid is eating healthy when they are really on a total junk diet. My friend had one mom who insisted her picky eater ate salad but when the child was given a fresh, green salad, he started bawling and saying he did not like it because he only eats the croutons dipped in ranch dressing. Eating fried bread cubes dipped in dressing is not eating a salad – that is eating junk.

Another common parental food lie revolves around allergies. They do not lie about allergies the child actually has, but rather, they lie about foods they do not want the child to have. I have had parents who were against using commercial cow milk, declaring their kid allergic, but insisting they could have grass-fed cow milk. Sometimes the parent will lie about allergies because they really want their child to have expensive food substitutions they cannot afford at home.

Sometimes parents will lie about what they are feeding their baby and how much. They will lie about the advice or direction their pediatrician gave them regarding feeding. When the formula baby ages and starts eating eight-ounce bottles, the parents want them to back off the formula and eat table food because the table food is included in the price of childcare. They want to supply less formula for daycare so they have more for the baby at home. They know the baby is easier to deal with if they have a full bottle when they get home and before bed. They want to use the formula they purchase at home and be skimpy with the formula they provide for childcare.

I do not allow parents to decide the amounts of formula I use in care. I follow the food program guidelines and require parents to bring the maximum serving size for each meal in my home. I do not allow baby or table food to substitute for the calories needed in the formula. If they are going to swap formula-calories for food-calories, they have to do that on their own time.

Sometimes you will see this with breastfed babies if the mom is struggling to produce enough milk for the baby. She may offer too little milk and want the provider to step up the table food. Many breastfeeding mothers do not want their baby to be supplemented with formula so they turn to food to make up the difference. Food intake for a baby under the age of one consists of a very small amount of calories each day. Food cannot be swapped out because it does not contain the high fat and protein the baby needs from formula and breast milk.

Sometimes these parents will go to their doctor and get a note saying the baby should have more food than is recommended by the federal food guidelines. I am more than happy to comply as long as the formula and breast milk amounts are not decreased as a result of the increase in food.

Developmentally Delayed Child Lying

It is very difficult to discuss with parents that their child is normal. Most parents do not want to discuss normal. They are often new to parenting and they do not have an accurate frame of reference to compare their child to other children.

Discussing normal does not go over too well. Discussing development delays is a universal bomb. There is such a wide breadth of normal in human babies, so I take a wait and see approach unless I feel there is something medically wrong with the child. If developmental issues are nearing the far end of the spectrum, I begin bringing them up to the parents.

Sometimes parents start to sense something wrong when they see younger children in their family, friends and public passing their child in developmental milestones. They often refer to their child as lazy or stubborn. Parents go through a stage of loss when reality is slapping them upside the head. The first stage is denial. They will state the child does or does not do something at home that the provider knows darn well is not true.

I am gifted in Toddlerese. I can understand the most garbled toddler speak because I have had so many toddlers dinging my eardrums for three decades. Once I had a little girl who had profound developmental delays. Other than Nan Nan, I could not understand a word she said. The mom kept telling stories about how she said she loved my house and loved the other kids. She would tell me stories of what the kid said we did. I told the mom I had never heard her talking like that. In fact, I never heard her say three words together. The mom insisted the child was talking in paragraphs. I was starting to doubt my mad skills because the girl did make a ton of sounds I could not decipher. I finally asked the mom to videotape the child and let me watch it when she came in the next day. I told her to just put her phone up on the table and let it record while they were eating supper.

Once I threw the gauntlet down and asked for proof, the fantastical stories stopped. The poor kid FINALLY got evaluated and her speech was so delayed, it literally was so far off the radar that it was not measurable. Speech therapy is the first service to which parents will normally agree. It opened up the other areas of delay within the speech evaluation and the additional services began.

I have had parents tell me a child could walk three months before I saw it. I have had children who could not crawl until after the age of one and the parent swore the child was zooming around the house like Dash from the Incredibles. Now that most parents have cell phones with the ability to videotape, there is not any reason for them to not capture the skill on tape so you can see it. Ask for it. If they start making excuses and then drop it, you will know they are lying.

Behavior at Home Lying

Children are very different at home than they are in childcare. It is a given that they are more comfortable with their parents. Many children keep it together during the day, but once they are with their parents they become whiny, clingy and demanding. They are more likely to act out when they are with their parents because it is safer and the child has a higher chance of the parents succumbing to their demands.

When the provider has behavioral issues with a child, the parents will often deny the behavior is happening at home. Some parents will insist their child is perfectly happy and well-mannered on their watch and any untoward behavior seen at the daycare is due to how the provider or other kids treat their child.

With infants, the most common discrepancy is in how much and when the baby cries. The parents may claim the child is not fussy at their house when the provider is claiming the child cries all or most of the day. Usually the crying is not because the baby misses the parents, but rather, the parents are able to afford the baby one-to-one care that cannot be replicated in a group setting. If the provider could hold, walk, rock and play solely with the baby all day, the crying would not be an issue.

Sometimes the baby does have anxiety about being away from the parents, but it does not take very long for the human baby to adapt to a loving, attentive caregiver who is meeting their basic needs. Once the baby has been in care a couple of weeks he should adjust to a new adult. When the crying persists past the first two weeks, it is important to get a very specific run down of what the parents do to address crying at home. If the answer is that they do one-to-one care, then the adults need to come to terms with the fact that the baby is going to be very different at daycare. If the baby needs their own adult then it is time to switch care providers.

If the parent denies doing one-to-one care, they imply that the provider does not know how to take care of babies and may blame the provider for the baby's unhappiness. The parent may be lying because they do not want to change childcare providers, hire a nanny or have the ability to afford staying home with the child. If the parent insists the baby is not fussy at home and they are content to self-soothe and self-entertain, the best solution is to concede that the baby would be better off with someone else who can provide an environment closer to what the parent offers at home. It does not pay to imply the parents are being untruthful because it does not matter either way. The only way for the baby to adjust is to have the truth out on the table. The parents must accept that the baby is going to cry a lot or they are going to have to change the way they are caring for the baby at home so he can acclimate to a group care environment where he is not offered one-to-one, minute-to-minute care. If the baby is fine at home without one-to-one care and the provider's home is not right for the baby, then the baby should go elsewhere.

Previous Care Lying

Lying about where the child previously attended childcare is common with parents of babies who cry constantly. It is also common with parents who have violent and aggressive kids.

Most providers will not take a child who has been terminated from two or more daycares. The parent of a difficult child will admit to being terminated only once: after the first termination. For subsequent terminations they lie as they find it difficult to find a provider who will take them as clients. When they cannot find a willing provider, parents often claim the previous caregiver was a relative. Once the child starts daycare, the truth will surface as the parents answer provider concerns by claiming the child did not do that in the previous daycare. If the provider is patient she will eventually hear about all the previous daycares.

Violence and Destruction of Property Lying

Infant behavior can be aggressive and occasionally violent once the child becomes mobile. A baby will try biting, pinching, scratching and hair pulling on the mom first. If the infant begins to sow the seeds of getting physical with the provider or other babies, the provider should inform the parents it is happening and has to stop. If the parent lies and says the baby is not doing these things at home, be very suspicious. It is an extremely rare baby that does not attempt these behaviors on the mother long before anyone else.

If the mother does not put the kibosh on the behavior, the baby will try it on the provider. It is important to watch how the baby is with the mom on drop-off and pick-up. If he is getting physical with her at home, he will often try it at the high energy time of arrival and departure. If you see it, say something immediately. Let the mom know he cannot do it at your house.

The mom may refer to slapping as patting, biting as kisses, clawing as clinging, etc. Do not allow her to change the intent with words. You know biting when you see it. You know hair pulling and slapping. It usually starts at around nine months, but it can end immediately if the mom does a hard fast "NO!" each and every time.

With breastfed babies you can have a situation where you do not see the baby in the act of getting physical if you do not host breastfeeding sessions at your house. It is becoming increasingly more common for breastfed babies to be allowed to get handsy when they are feeding. The baby is allowed to twist, pinch, squeeze, tug, massage and claw at the opposite breast and the nipple he is feeding from. If the mom stops the behavior when the baby is being nursed to sleep, the baby wakes up. Breastfeeding moms sometimes allow it because they do not want the baby to wake up. You can always tell these babies because when you are bottle feeding them they are trying to claw at your arm, pull your hair or twist the fabric of your sleeve.

If you experience this while feeding the baby, inform the mom and let her know he cannot do that with you. There are breastfeeding necklaces moms can wear to give the baby something to hold onto and manipulate while feeding. They do not work well because the baby wants the skin to skin feel of the breast and opposing nipple. Babies do not need to suck AND do another repetitive motion, soothing behavior at the same time. Sucking a bottle or a nipple is enough repetitive motion for soothing and gratification. They do not need to do MORE. If it bothers or hurts you, tell the mom to stop allowing it. She may be willing to endure the painful behavior, but she should not expect you to do the same. She may lie and deny the baby does it because it is awkward to admit a baby is doing this to her body. Whether she admits it or not, it has to stop.

There are some babies who are extremely violent when they are not getting their way. They scream and go after the provider and other kids. I have heard terrible stories of providers who have babies chasing after them only to get at their legs to scratch, bite and claw. They target any other baby or child who is within reach. They often go after the hair and back of the other babies. Even when they are being held they will not settle down.

I call these babies "rage babies." It is a rare behavior in a baby, but it does happen. I know one provider who terminated a ten-month old baby after he attacked her own child, leaving deep bruises and bite marks. He would make a beeline straight for her child and would climb on top of her and punch her with a closed fist. When being pulled off of the other kids he would kick and head butt the provider.

The parents were furious with the provider and refused to even look at the welt marks on her toddler's back. The parents reported her to the State when she did an immediate termination. She kept pictures of her daughter to show the State because she knew they would be coming around shortly after she let the baby go. She found out a few months later that she was the third childcare provider for this ten-month old and he had been terminated twice before for violence. The parents lied to her when they interviewed and told her he had been home with grandma. They lied by omission when they did not forewarn her of his aggression.

The toddler, preschool and school-aged child can cause serious damage to the provider, other children and property. When confronting parents about their child's violence and destruction, they tend to minimize it. Some parents will outright lie about what the child does when they are caring for him. The reason most parents lie about violence and destruction is because they want to imply the child is only having the problem at childcare so the problem needs to be fixed at childcare. Denying takes them out of the loop of having to deal with the child. It also absolves them of having to pay for things the child destroys.

These parents deny that their child hits, slaps, kicks, pulls hair, spits or bites. They may look the provider in the eye and tell them the child does not do that at home despite the provider being witness to this very behavior towards the parent at drop-off and pick-up. In the walk from her house to their car, she has seen the child run from the parent and then attack them when captured. She sees the battle as the child bucks and kicks when he is being put into the car seat. Older children take joy in unbuckling themselves to run off and start the game over again.

When the parent implies the behavior only occurs at daycare, they must be terminated. They are a danger to the provider's business and freedom. It is only on the day of termination the parent will admit to some problems they have at home. It is only then they apologize for their child hurting another kid or the provider. They do not do it because they are now comfortable with sharing the truth or because they feel badly that someone was hurt; they do it because they need daycare tomorrow.

There are some parents who truly do not have a problem with their child being violent or destructive in daycare. These parents believe their child is the King or Queen and the daycare provider and children are their subjects. Kingdoms go to war and, with war, there will be casualties. They believe their child rules because he is a natural leader, powerful and deserving of the alpha position in the house. They look at the provider as his servant and expect her to tolerate the behavior because she is being paid. They pronounce all of the behavior as being normal for his age.

The idea that a vicious child is normal for his age is a slap to the face in every area of growth and development EXCEPT violence and damage to property. This parent will throw out the word "normal" like candy at a Mardi Gras parade when called to the carpet about their child's violent and destructive behavior.

Daycare Whispers…

Be firm with parents about safe sleeping.

Do not allow parents to change your schedule with the child so they can have an early, easy bedtime.

Parents care about the health of the other children BEFORE their child becomes ill. Precious few care about the others AFTER their child has become ill.
Every child must be fully awake and active when they come into your home. Do not accept sleeping children and do an assessment of them right when they arrive.

Do not get roped into giving medication the parents can do on their own clock.

Require that breastfed babies eat a full bottle in front of you within two days of starting care. Do not take a parent's word that the baby is nipple trained.

Have the parent videotape skillsets the child has at home, but does not show at daycare.

If the child has been in multiple childcare arrangements before coming to you, the parents may lie about the number of caregivers and why the care was terminated.

Watch how the child behaves with the mother at drop-off and pick-up. If he is violent with her, he will be violent in your childcare.

You do not have to host violence. Violence is never normal.

The "Boss of Me" Parent

I have been doing home childcare for two decades and try as I might, I can never find a daycare parent who will be my boss. I want a whole house full of boss parents, but I cannot find a single one.

Now, I am not hard pressed to find a house full of parents who want to boss me around. That is easy enough. That is the fun part of being the boss. What I cannot find are boss parents who want the financial responsibility of being my boss.

How I long for a boss who pays me minimum wage for every hour I work and time-and-a-half for every hour over eight. I want the half-hour break where I get to leave the house every eight hours. I dream of them paying the employer portion of my social security and Medicare taxes and the most beloved FUTA Federal Unemployment Tax.

Federal Holidays, come to Mama! Columbus Day and Washington's Birthday, I heart you. I will take them off paid or be paid time-and-a-half - whichever works best for my boss. No more quarterly taxes for me because the boss-parent gets to withhold and deliver my federal, state and social security portion.

The boss parent would be on the fry for a portion of my health insurance too. If I could get three or four bosses to pay twenty percent each, I could cough up the rest, no sweat. My insurance is over a grand a month so each boss would only have to dish out a couple of hundred dollars more a month. That is a small price to pay to keep me healthy.

I would only have to keep three kids and you can be sure they would all be singletons. Minimum wage from three sets of boss parents would be enough for me to live quite comfortably. I could take a fourth kid if I wanted to hire a minimum wage staff assistant. She could handle the awesome foursome by herself and I would not have to work at all.

All of these employee benefits would make it worth it to be bossed around in my own home. The benefit I want so badly... the one I dream of night and day... is the unemployment. I think I should have t-shirts made that say, "Boss Me" on the front and "Woota to da FUTA" on the back.

I want a paycheck for eighteen months after every single kid leaves my house. I would be thrilled with sixty percent of the income. I would do a happy dance when I received a termination notice. I would not be in a big fat hurry to fill a slot if I knew I could get that much money and not have a single expense for caring for the kids. If I could get all three parents to fire me at the same time I could live quite comfortably!

Daycare parents becoming the employer of the home providers would categorically change home childcare. It will never happen, but it is incredibly fun thinking about it. It is frustrating to deal with a parent who thinks they are your boss but is not willing to do the not-so-fun parts of being an employer.

Home childcare is a unique business in that each client represents a substantial part of the total income of the business. The smaller the capacity of the childcare, the higher the income per child. If a provider has six kids full time, each child represents approximately 17 percent of the provider's livelihood.

On the parents end, the daycare bill is often second only to their housing bill as their biggest monthly expense. If they have multiple children it can be the largest bill. Because the parents pay such a huge part of their income for daycare, they often feel they have the right to run the daycare show. When you couple the math with the fact that the service provided is the care of a child, the expectation that the provider do as they are told escalates even higher.

Parents innately believe they have the say about everything related to their children. When they have someone caring for their child AND are paying a large portion of their salary for it, they automatically assume they can and should control the daycare provider and business.

Parents do not go into a childcare center with the same mindset. If the center has two hundred kids the parent is a mere half percent of the total income of the business. They could be paying more for the center care, resulting in an even larger chunk of their family income, but they do not view themselves as the boss of that business. They may feel that as the parent they can influence the decisions about the individual care of the child, but they know they must do that in accordance to the policies of the business and the approval of the owners and directors. When the center child leaves, it is a mere blip on the financial radar of a center. The center's staff is not affected financially. They get paid whether that child is in the slot or not.

A home daycare provider losing the income of one kid of five or eight is going to suffer. It is within that cycle the parent believes they have the power to determine the work and allowances offered by the home provider. They are the boss because they control the care of their child, pay a large portion of their income and represent a large percentage of the provider's income.

The provider views this situation much differently. The weekly salary may be substantial for each child, but the hourly rate of care is not. It does not make sense that a person paying three dollars an hour for the hard, hard work of caring for kids gets to be the boss, too. Out of the money the provider earns there are large expenses that chip away at her net profit. After she pays for the cost of operating the business, she is left with a fraction of that three dollars an hour. Housing alone takes at least a third of every dollar.

The daycare provider also has competing interests. What one boss wants may directly interfere with what the other bosses want. These competing forces go to war in the areas of health, safety, one-to-one care, outdoor care and education. One parent may want their child to be outside playing all day while another wants their baby inside being rocked during the nap. One parent may want a breakfast service at 9 a.m., an hour after the other children have finished eating. Most parents are very comfortable having their ill child being cared for by the provider. The other parents do not want that kid under the same roof as their child.

And on and on it goes... There can only be one boss in a home childcare and that boss MUST be the owner of the business, not the customers. The provider must insist that every client accessing her services understand that they are customers, not employers. If she allows multiple bosses to dictate her business, she will fail and it will happen quickly. The average home provider lasts two years. Not enforcing a clear and respected position as a self-employed business owner is the most predominant reason a home childcare goes out of business.

Managing the parent who wants to be the boss is a difficult aspect of the business. I cut some slack to this parent when I first meet them. I understand the genesis of their belief that they have the right to dictate everything about their child's care by virtue of being the parent. That concept is woven into the fabric of parenting from conception on by baby book authors and society as a whole. It is a mindset that goes out the window once the child goes into public school, but this mindset does not change until after the provider-parent relationship ends. School is also free so the average parent is thrilled to not have to pay for their kid to be taken care of while they are at work. When money is removed from the equation, concessions are easier to tolerate.

I empathize with the percentage of income the parent must relinquish for my service. I paid for summer care for my son when he was in elementary school and it was my second largest bill. Hated it.

I face the inevitable conversation in our first meeting. I use the words "self-employed" numerous times when I go through the policies of the childcare. I refer to the work I do as a service. Then

I use the concept of "offering service" as a way to either agree to care for their child a certain way or to take a pass on the opportunity to care for their child. I use the phrases "I do not provide that service" or "I will provide that service for an additional fee" to say no to the wishes they have that are not standard in the care I offer.

If a parent requests their child to be up during a nap, I say, "I do not provide that service." If a parent wants me to hold their baby while she sleeps I say, "I do not provide that service". If a parent wants a schedule change I say, "I provide that service for an additional fee of $X". I do not spend time judging whether the request is reasonable or in the best interest of the child. That is the parent's job, not mine. My role is to agree to provide it or decline the offer to provide it.

There are situations that arise where the parent does not ask and the request for services is mistakenly assumed as a task or event I should host. For example, a child may be punching, scratching and biting his mother at my front door. The parent may believe it is my job to allow this on my property. In these situations, I have to define the parental wish and then declare whether or not I provide the service. In the case of a kid being violent on my property, I would say, "I cannot allow a child to be violent on my property. If you want to allow him to be violent you must leave. I do not provide the service of hosting violence."

It sounds wordy, but there is not a nice way to tell parents that you do not want kids being wicked to their mother on your land. My words do not indicate whether or not the parent SHOULD allow it, they are to clarify with the parents that it just cannot be done HERE. I do not have an opinion; I just confirm whether or not I provide the service.

A parent may want to hang out before or after their scheduled daycare day. They often believe they have the right to be in the home any time there are kids in the house. I have to tell them I do not allow parents in the playroom, parents parenting their child on my property or parent conferencing beyond the paid daycare day. I understand a parent wanting these services, but I do not provide them. If they need that in their daycare relationship, my services will not meet their needs.

This approach works beautifully in defining a provider as a self-employed, service provider. It allows issues to be brought up and addressed without judging the parental want. I do not try to tell them what to do. I just tell them what I will do for the fee they are contracted to pay.

One last note about parent's natural inclination that the provider is their employee… The parent is paying a good portion of their income for this service, but they cannot really envision it or qualify it like they do their other bills such as rent, car payments or food. Childcare is intangible and does not net them anything other than they do not have the child with them for ten hours a day. They often believe the job is easy for the provider and the expense to the provider to have the child in her home is very small or nonexistent. Their child is small, does not eat much, does not take up a lot of room or need much.

They believe the provider already has to pay for her house, car, equipment, etc., so their child is not a burden worth such a huge amount of money monthly. This same parent brings their child to childcare every single day they are off work because the child is too difficult to manage while running errands and relaxing around the house. They convince themselves that for them caring for the child is hard, but for the provider it is easy.

This mindset leads them to feel cheated every week. They want something for their money other than the easy care of their child. They want something more for themselves out of the deal. This parent wants additional time with the provider and if they can work it out, time with the provider before and after daycare hours. This desire to get more for their money usually manifests itself by them wanting time and attention. They hang out at the provider's house, call during off-hours and text the provider during her time off. Having that kind of access makes them feel like they are not only the boss, but the recipient of getting their money's worth.

The provider does not set fees with excessive parent conferencing included. She calculates in a few minutes a day at drop-off and pick-up and an occasional meeting to discuss the child. She never considers having the parents hanging out long after the kid is off the clock. She does not charge for texting and weekend communication.

When the parent requires communication outside of the daycare hours, they feel they are getting what they are owed and the provider feels like she is working overtime for nothing. The provider's resentment for being forced to tolerate or address this behavior with parents causes conflict that can fester over time.

The best thing I have found to put a stop to being roped into additional services is to define and address them as services. You have to be bold enough to say, "Dad, I see you would like to hang out after hours, but I do not provide that service. I am charging you for the hours of seven to four and I do not allow parents in the playroom." Being that specific and attaching money to the conversation shows the parent that you are the boss and you decide what you do and do not want to offer.

If a parent boldly states they are your boss and they expect you to do as they say, you can offer to agree to that arrangement as long as they are willing to take on the financial aspects of being an employer. Once they realize they have to take on the part of the boss relationship that costs them way more money and time, they will quickly reconsider. Being the boss is not all it is cracked up to be unless you get to be the boss for free. And, again, I do not provide that service.

Daycare Whispers…

Be your own boss.

You know your business best and you know what's best for your business. Have confidence in that.

Be understanding that a new client may view the relationship differently. You have to teach them the "boss" ropes.

Businesses do not allow customers to be the boss. Just because the services are about children it does not mean their parents get to assume the boss position because they have a child at stake. Other businesses that offer services and goods geared toward children do not allow it and neither should you.

When a parent is asking for something you do not offer whether they ask with words or intent, use the phrase "I do not provide that service."

The Picky Parent

I enjoy picky parents. I have made a great living off of them for two decades. Because I am a nurse, I draw the overcautious, newbie moms who are in fear every second of their child's life. I, too, live in paralyzing fear of a child being injured or hurt in my care, so we are a match made in daycare heaven.

Picky parents are exact. I function well with rule-governed expectations. The parent knows what they want and looks specifically for that kind of care. When I interview them I can decide if what they want is a service I provide. If either of us should decide it will not work, it is no harm, no foul.

Being picky is a good thing. You do not have to worry about the parent not expressing how they feel about each aspect of the child's care. They want a specific diet, exercise, sleep arrangements, supervision, cleanliness and a manageable group of children per adult. They are upfront without apology on their expectations.

I was blessed to get a picky parent at the beginning of my career. We are friends to this day. She worked in management her entire career and was used to juggling multiple staff and the pressures of a retail business. She was very kind about expressing what she wanted for her son. She did not waiver under pressure. She was an experienced mother of a child with two much older siblings so she had the ease that comes with a seasoned parent. She made me want to get better at my job. Never miss an opportunity to learn from your clients.

Her two older daughters worked for me and her son was in my daycare for ten years. This long term relationship had many moving parts as her son and daughters aged. It worked because we both had high standards for all three children and we presented a united front for the care of her son and the expectation that her teenagers would be good workers. When problems came up, and there were many between the three kids, we tackled them as a business and as parents. She kept every promise she made to me and honored me with bonuses, supplies and gifts for my childcare and my son.

When dealing with my other daycare parents, I modeled what she did with me when we had a conflict. I liked the way she talked to me so I copied it when I talked to parents about problems. She was soft spoken, paused to give me a chance to talk, gave great eye contact, rephrased what I said and ended every conversation with, "this is what we are going to try."

I learned from her that pickiness is not personal. It is just a high standard set for the relationship. When problems arise you have a foundation of respect for the mutual agreement you made in the beginning. It makes problem solving simple.

I am not referring to pickiness that is unrealistic and changes constantly. That is unhealthy and feels attention seeking when you are on the receiving end. I will not allow parents to change the game as we go along because they want to get their "I am the boss of you" on. I will not be a party to being forced to give the parent more attention than I give their kids.

I am referring to a parent who invests in learning about what is good, healthy care of a newborn, infant, toddler and preschooler and wants you to join in rearing a healthy, balanced member of society.

There is a difference between picky and "nit" picky. A picky parent serves broad general themes of care. A nitpicky parent wallows in the minutia of every event that does not fall in their favor or their child's favor. I do not abide by nitpicky. These parents seize every opportunity to point out a provider's shortcomings and constantly engage the provider to surrender and do as they are told. A parent who treats me like a sibling they want to overpower and put in his place will not be welcome.

The nitpicky parent wants to be involved fully in the activities the child does every day. They want the provider to do the things they do not like doing with the child which is usually in outdoor play, healthy eating and the grueling education of the Pookie. They may demand proof that the provider is working on daily education of writing and reading. They want the child outside so they do not have to do the boring outdoor supervision. They also do not want the child in front of a screen. They want the child to be up and playing and doing school so they can have the child in front of the TV or a tablet on their clock.

When you really look at what the nitpicky parent focuses on, it is almost exactly the opposite of what they do at home. There is an element of "do the right thing in daycare so I can do the wrong thing at home." To them, this means the kid has a balance of the good and the bad. It makes them feel better about them doing the unhealthy things with the child if they know the child has been filled with goodness all day.

An example would be parents requesting the provider stop allowing the child to have a pacifier (right thing) because the child is suffering speech delay and mouth malformations from having it in constantly so that the parent can use it exclusively at home (wrong thing). The parent believes it is better to have some time to correct these problems when the child is not using it, but they only want that time to be when someone else has the kid.

They sometimes want to "do the wrong thing to avoid doing anything at all." This is common in limited or no nap requests. The parent wants the provider to keep the very exhausted kid up all day long (wrong thing) even though the child is suffering so the parent can put the kid to bed shortly after arriving at home (do nothing at all).

The picky parent has a grand plan with a goal of a well-rounded healthy kid. They pick a provider who is as close to them as possible so the child has an easy transition between both houses and remains constant in behavior and growth and development.

The nitpicky parent wants the child to have the best when they are at daycare so the child gets the best at least half the time.

Know the difference between picky and nitpicky. Do not shy away from exacting parents. Be confident in the work you do and work side by side to raise up a great kid. Do not take their involvement as a personal affront. Shut the nitpicky parent down. They will drive you insane with their pettiness. Set firm limits on what is up for discussion and involvement and what is not. Expect them to behave when they are bringing up issues and send a clear message that you will not divest your energies into little things just to keep their money.

Daycare Whispers...

Picky parents can be a blessing because they are very upfront as to what they are looking for. If you do not offer it, they are not upset, they just move on.

Pickiness is not personal. It is just a high standard set for the relationship.

The picky parent has a grand plan to end up with a well-rounded healthy kid.

A nitpicky parent seizes every opportunity to point out a provider's shortcomings and constantly engages the provider to surrender and do as they are told.

A nitpicky parent wants the provider to do the things the parent does not like doing with the child.

What a nitpicky parent focuses on in the childcare relationship is almost exactly the opposite of what they do at home.

The Attachment Parent

I have seen many parenting styles cycle over the three and a half decades of my childcare experience. Currently, attachment parenting has become popular. This style of parenting often includes breastfeeding, baby wearing and co-sleeping. There are other aspects, but these three components are the primary ones that can affect the child in childcare.

I will go into greater detail regarding the care of infants and toddlers who are attachment parented in the Doing Daycare series. In this installment, I will just speak to the attachment parent in accessing and maintaining a childcare partnership.

The attachment parent comes to the daycare table with specific negotiations about how much adult the baby or child will get every day. They want to know what the provider does and what they allow. They may believe they get to decide what the provider can offer their child. They know their baby cries at home and what they do to quickly address and stop the crying. They have a hard time envisioning how the provider will mimic what they do when they have any other children in the home. These foundational concerns can nearly always be traced to avoidance of their child crying.

The attachment parent may use sleeping methods at home that are illegal for the provider to use in care because they are dangerous. They may want their child to sleep in a wrap, swing, bouncer seat, with a blanket to the face or on a surface where the provider can lie with the child. They may want the infant to sleep on their belly.

The child who is used to being carried, nursed for comfort and slept with has a very different experience in childcare. A parent may believe that she can give permission to the provider for the child to sleep in the same manner they sleep at their own home, but this is not acceptable. In my State, the parent cannot give permission for these methods as they are against the law. Providers need to study and comply with their State's sleep regulations.

Most State sleep regulations do not allow for any of these methods because children die of positional asphyxia in higher numbers than when they are on their backs in empty cribs or playpens. The parents are allowed to take the risk of their child dying when using these sleep methods, but the States do not allow the provider to take that risk. They also do not allow parents to give permission for the provider to use these methods. Parents cannot give a provider permission to do the wrong thing.

The attachment parent is attracted to providers who offer to carry the baby in a sling all or most of the day. The simple math of this is if the baby is physically attached to the provider, they will have the provider's attention every second. The parent knows the baby prefers to be held and this type of holding allows the providers hands to be free to care for the other kids.

Attachment parents sometimes subscribe to the Baltic amber necklaces as an external method of decreasing teething pain. The evidence supporting the claim that these necklaces actually affect teething pain is testimonial, rather than scientific, evidence. The amber necklace has become a status symbol and an instant identifier of the crunchy granola parent. Because they are a choking hazard, many providers cannot allow the baby to wear them in care. The parent may only consider providers who do.

The parent may be looking for a provider to become very invested into breast milk management. If the baby is free fed at the breast, uses the breast for suckling during the day and sleeps suckling the mother's nipple all night long, the parent wants to negotiate the care that will come as close to this as possible for the baby. Managing breast milk a couple of tablespoons at a time is very time-consuming because convection heating is labor intensive. If the baby will not drink room temperature milk, this may be so time-consuming the provider cannot manage it.

This style of care is hard to complement, but I have seen an upsurge of providers offering to manage breast milk with on demand feedings throughout infancy and to wrap and carry the baby. The provider may offer to stay with the baby when the baby sleeps and maintain physical contact like patting the butt or rocking the crib back and forth. They may also fudge the rules and allow the baby to sleep while eating and rocking.

The methods the parents use at home to avoid crying are extremely time-consuming, require a massive amount of adult interaction and are often illegal in childcare. The parent believes the child needs this type of care and they search for a provider who also believes. It is difficult to find someone with a group care setting who will do this type of care for a few dollars an hour. It is more like nanny care than daycare care.

The parent wants to pay for the childcare portion, but wants the attachment care portion done with "in kind" support because the provider feels it is right and good. This means the provider does the labor intensive care for free in addition to the regular care they would normally give to a child in group care.

The biggest problem is that the parent believes they should be able to decide how their baby is cared for and they want to "permission out" the care that is illegal or unsafe. If the provider refuses to do as the parent wishes, they will look for a different provider. These parents often end up with an unregistered, unlicensed, informal stay-at-home mom with one or two kids who also does attachment parenting with her own children. This is often a match made in daycare heaven.

The parent who is practicing attachment parenting may be a very tired client. The type of care they give their baby often leads to them being up multiple times in the night long past the newborn stage of the baby's life. When they are home on maternity leave it is easier for them to "work" around the clock. Time does not matter when you are not on an employee schedule, but when the mother goes back to work she is working all day and night. Attachment moms continue the newborn style care for many more months and often years. If they have a second child, it is exponentially more difficult to be up both all night and all day.

When you work with a client who is literally exhausted all the time, it can make for a strained provider/parent relationship. Requests to keep the baby up for longer periods of the day are very common. The mother hopes the baby will be more tired at night if he or she is up most of the day. This does not work well because the baby is also up a significant amount of the night feeding and suckling while co-sleeping. With the continuous feedings, numerous diaper changes and burping also occur.

It takes a bit of understanding and compassion to work with clients who are tired to the bone all the time. Offering sleeping advice or different methods will usually upset the mother. It is sometimes best to stay out of it and let them figure it out.

I do not have a tremendous amount of experience with attachment moms. They started showing up on my radar about six or seven years ago. I think they get a lot of guff they do not deserve, so I try not to interject my own feelings about their parenting style unless I am specifically asked and given a promise they will not take it too hard if they do not like my suggestions. I warn them not to ask questions they do not want the answer to.

I believe their parenting style comes from a good place. I would much rather work with a family that is trying their hardest to net the most excellent children within a bonded family, than a family that puts their children in the back of the stadium without a care about learning to properly care for and raise them. Attachment parents do their homework and surround themselves with like-minded parents for support. They are very conscientious about trying to find providers who are on the same page. It is a hard row to hoe because group care and attachment care are a polar opposite.

Daycare Whispers…

Follow best practices and State regulations for acceptable sleep positions for infants. When in doubt, contact your State agency.

Baltic Amber Necklaces are a choking hazard.

Do not agree to more one-to-one care than you can realistically do.

Be sensitive to the mother's fatigue but do not compromise a normal daycare sleep schedule for the baby to sleep more at night.

The State Paid Parent

Every state has programs available to subsidize low-income families to pay for childcare. Working with state subsidy clients is a very different business experience than working with private pay clients. I have had wonderful experiences with a number of state-paid parents. They utilized the program for its original intent and maintained a stable job or completed an education program. They moved on to become contributors to the system that funded them when they needed it. I have also had a few bad experiences and have counseled a number of providers who have had horrible experiences. I will only speak to the dynamics of dealing with the parents in this section as each state has a different financial arrangement with providers who take assistance.

I want to disclose upfront that I have serious issues with childcare funding. My main concern is that the recipient is able to apply for funding without proving they have attempted to get child support from the non-custodial parent. I believe we should require they go to Daddy before they go to Uncle Sam. Other entitlement programs require the parent to seek child support and I cannot understand why this is not required for childcare assistance. I also believe this funding should be time-limited and should not extend to future children once the recipient has received assistance for existing children. When it is offered for multiple children in one family it can easily exceed what the recipient makes in their job. It is a very expensive cash-like benefit that is given without strings or expectations to repay.

One of the biggest frauds in childcare assistance is the mother claiming the father of the child does not live with the family. The father's income is not included in the financial application and the mother is not required to prove the father does not live with the family or that the family does not benefit from his income. If the father's income was counted, the family would not qualify. There is little the State does to insure the applicant is being honest about the one thing that would automatically disqualify them.

Childcare assistance scams are pervasive. Soon after enrollment, the provider will find themselves in a difficult position as they become more knowledgeable about the family. When she realizes the mom has lied or not disclosed the father being with or rejoining the family, she has already given the slots to the family. It is hard to take the step to turn the family in when she is not privy to the application, but common sense and simple math tell her the family should not be within the income limits. Providers should attempt to vet this through the interview before the client starts. If the mom is shady about answering questions about where the dad lives, but indicates he will drop off or pick up daily, you have a pretty good idea they are running game. If it is too risky to get involved, it is best to walk away before you are put in a difficult position of needing to report a possible fraud.

State paid clients have inherent, common issues that work their way into the childcare relationship. The families are low-income and often lead an unstable home and work life. The care of the state paid child can be challenging because the resources available to the client are different than the average, middle class, private pay family. It is not unusual to find the state paid clients are actually better off financially than the private pay family. If they access all the public assistance available these days, it is possible a state paid family with multiple children is actually better off financially than your private paid families. They can easily have more available cash at the end of the month than families who are paying for their own rent, food, college loans, health care and childcare. What they do with that cash may be very different than private pay clients.

The monetary differences you see between the families are in the life expenses not given for free to the subsidy parent. These are vehicles, diapers, clothing and, sometimes, housing. Free housing is available, but access to it can take years. WIC is available to supplement formula, but around the baby's sixth month, the formula given for free is not enough to cover the child's monthly need. The parent must spend their food stamps or income for the balance. Free phones are available, but they are very limited in service and are mostly used as a secondary phone. I mention these because the life expenses that are not given for free or are only partially free affect the care of the child and the management of the parent.

State-funded recipients have a higher turnover in employment than private pay clients. They often work low paying jobs and as a worker who will accept a low wage, they are in demand in the workforce. It is easy for them to switch jobs if they are fired or become disenfranchised with their work. Some states offer childcare while the recipient seeks a new job. Some states only verify the employment of the recipient every six months. This can lead to recipients maintaining a job for the enrollment period for assistance and then quitting their job after being approved. This gives them the opportunity to have childcare for months without working. This is illegal, but the provider and state may be unaware the recipient is not employed. If the recipient is determined and willing to take the risk, they can work a couple of months out of the year and have childcare the entire year. If they have all their basic needs met with free housing, food, utility subsidy and medical care, they have very little need for cash.

Unfortunately, the life expenses they have to spend their income on can affect the child and provider. If the client does not have money for diapers, formula, clothing or car maintenance, the childcare relationship is strained. Providers need the child to have supplies, be in clean clothing that fits, have adequate amounts of formula for the older infants and to be present at daycare so the provider can bill for the day.

The childcare subsidy recipient often has little to no cash reserves. Unexpected car repairs can put the recipient and the provider out of a job. I have lost state paid clients over a blown out tire they were unable to repair which resulted in them missing work and losing their job.

An unstable living arrangement can sometimes force the recipient to move to an area that is too far away from a provider. I have found the recipients who are already on free housing to be much more stable than the ones who are living with family, friends or a father of one or more of the children. Living with a grandparent is even more stable than living with parents, friends or father.

There is a direct correlation between longevity in a relationship with a parent who lives and works close to the home childcare. The expenses of operating a car are greatly diminished if the parent is in close proximity. Also, the hours of care are less per day which naturally increases the hourly wage the provider nets if the funding is based on blocks of time as opposed to hourly.

One of the challenging aspects of working with fully funded childcare clients is the cash-like subsidy is quickly taken for granted. Once they are approved for funding, they do not respect the value of what they are getting or the responsibility they have to insure the provider gets paid and is aware of any changes that may disqualify the recipient. They want the free care, but the paperwork to continue the service often goes by the wayside. It is not unusual for them to postpone filing the necessary documents which can threaten the provider getting paid.

My state has an excellent online portal where providers can verify funding. It is very well maintained and the workers are easy to reach if you have billing questions. They identify any upcoming changes at the top of the screen to alert the provider that the funding is coming to an end. This helps so much in letting the parent know you know they have things they need to do. A little push in the right direction helps getting the parent to get documents in on time. A clear discussion that the child's care will end on a specific date if the parent does not comply allows the conversation to begin BEFORE the services are discontinued. If the provider makes it clear she will not provide service if the approval is not granted, the parent does not try to bring a child without funding.

Do not ever take a state paid clients word that they are funded – not even one time. I have known providers who accepted multiple children from a family relying solely on the parent's words who ended up getting stiffed for thousands of dollars before they realized the client was never approved. There are NO exceptions to this rule. Do not take the parent's word or even a worker's word. Take only the written word from the Notice of Decision.

There are other relationship dynamics that are inherent to working with someone who is getting something very expensive for free. The childcare "free" plus all the other low income "free" can net an entitled parent. The resources they receive for being low income are valuable when they first receive them, but are not really considered until the next time they have to reapply for them.

A provider working long hours for a few dollars an hour per kid can easily get jealous of the amount of financial help the parent is getting. They have a hard time listening to money complaints when their own tax dollars are paying for the funded clients food, shelter, childcare, health insurance and education. The provider considers how much better off her family would be if she divorced her husband and accessed the resources the recipient receives.

Childcare providers can become judgmental about the way the state paid client spends her money. If the recipient smokes, drives a nicer car, has a high dollar cellphone or the cash to eat out frequently, the provider compares her budgeted life and begrudges the client for how good she has it. When supplies are needed or the recipient does not have the co-pay, it causes tension because the provider feels what little the parent has to pay for should be easily given considering how much the parent is getting for free. The parent's perspective is that they would prefer for it all to be free and would like the provider to make the supplies available and not require the co-pay.

There is also a dynamic I have seen with state paid clients and providers when the client has multiple children in care. If the client has two or more children in care, they can easily be a third or half of the provider's total income. It does not take the state paid client long to realize the hold they have on the provider when they take up a good portion of the available slots. They know from previous experience with other providers that they are granted a lot of leeway because the provider does not want them to leave and take half of her family's income with them. You do not see this so much with only one state paid child in a family, but it becomes very common with two or more. In Iowa, the current rates would be about eleven hundred dollars a month for two state paid kids. This is a mortgage payment to most providers. It is serious money and the state paid client knows it.

So you have a weird dynamic. A state paid client has the power to access expensive services with money she did not earn. The money she receives may actually be a result of poor family planning, poor choice of men, poor work history and poor educational outcomes. The client could have a history of doing the wrong thing in all areas of their financial and family life and end up getting a reward of thousands of dollars per year in assistance.

They can also become the boss of the provider because they have a high dollar subsidy to bring to the table. It is often the only time in the recipient's life that they GET to be the boss. They did not earn their role as boss. They did not study for it or have monthly student loan payments to show for it. They did not work their way up the ladder to become the leader. They have access to this role because they have children they cannot provide for without someone else paying for it. This does not a great boss make.

A little power can go to anyone's head, but it can be disastrous when given to someone who hasn't earned it. The state paid client with multiple kids has a lot of power when she arrives with her brood to childcare, but the minute she walks out your door she often goes to a job where she is the lowest man on the totem pole and has to take orders and do undesirable work for low pay. The only time of her life where she is the top dog is in the childcare relationship. Some of these recipients take advantage of this position by expecting the provider to do parental care of their child, not keeping provider abreast of pending changes, expecting the provider to adapt with short notice, ignoring concerns of the provider by dismissing or arguing about them and never thanking or showing gratitude.

Some providers offer leniencies such as using extra hours, being late, coming early, taking sick kids, changing schedules, etc. because they will lose a large portion of her monthly income and have to fill slots if the parent pulls their kids. Most states do not pay for contracted termination notice time, so the day the parent pulls the child is the last day of income for the provider.

I want to reiterate that this is not the case with all state funded clients. I know there are recipients who work hard to better their life and are the victims of unforeseen life changes that put them in a position where they must ask for help. They are grateful and humble for the help they get. With these clients, the funding is often short lived because they do what it takes to get back on their feet. These recipients are out there on the childcare market, but sadly, they are quickly becoming extinct.

I have had success with having state paid clients in my business. I am very strict about who I will take with both private and state paid. I only allow a small percentage of my total daycare income to be taken up by state paid. I do not consider families with three or more children and only consider families with two children if the hours are a perfect fit for the rest of my schedule.

When I interview with the state-funded recipient I conduct myself very differently than I do with private pay. I spend a good portion of my time making sure I humanize myself to them. I want them to see me as a flesh and blood human being who is trying to provide for my child and make my own way.

When they come to my house they see a large house that is toy rich and nicely furnished. They see up-to-date electronics and expensive food. They can easily put me into the category of one who has and not one who needs. I want to dismantle that way of thinking. I want them to understand that I worked very long hours for a very long time to have all they see. I do not want them to think my success has been gifted to me. I want them to understand that I created this. I made this happen. I went to college and have devoted my entire adulthood to childcare in some fashion. I have because I do.

If they see me as someone who can afford to offer them leniency, they want me to be lenient. They are so used to having their financial and home deficiencies covered by someone else, they do not appreciate how terribly hard it is to be the one who does it on their own. They have not done it, so they do not get it.

I talk to them about the history of my childcare. I tell them about the sixteen years I worked double shifts, five days a week and the four years I worked around the clock seven days a week. I want them to know how many hours a week I work now to keep the business up and running. I explain to them that I have always been a single mom. I know how hard it is to raise a child completely alone and I know what it is like to be that child. I do not have empathy that extends to concessions because a parent is a single parent. I do not ask for them as one and I do not offer them as one.

It may seem that disclosing all of this would be counterintuitive to empowering the client to believe they are my boss. If I tell them I need money just like they do and that I depend on everyone's income to feed and house my own family, they may believe they have the upper hand because I need their money. I want them to understand I need the money, but also realize I do not need their money. I can get money without it being routed through them. I know what it is like to be poor and not have money. I am not willing to do that again.

Instead of them thinking they can run game with me because I need the money, I explain that because I need the money, I do not allow anyone to run game. See the difference? When the day comes that I have to let them go because their lifestyle and choices are making it impossible for me to have the money I need, I do it without a second thought. They understand my reaction to anything that means I get less money or no money because I have laid down this foundation of understanding.

I have techniques for bringing state paid clients into your daycare and making an excellent salary despite the lower market rate offered in most states. There are ways to work the money out to your advantage and keep state families long term.

One way I manage the financial relationship with the state paid client is that when I take on a state paid client I work three months before I submit a bill. My state allows billing as often as every two weeks or as seldom as once a year. I choose to start billing after I have three months in reserve. It is hard to work three months without a payday, but I do it because I want the salary available to cover my expenses if the client leaves without notice. I require a month's notice for each child in the private pay family. If a family has three children, I require a three-month notice of termination.

My state does not pay notice time for state-paid kids. I could possibly require the state paid client to contract that they will pay the notice time as I do the private pay clients, but pursuing it would be like getting blood from a turnip. If I was successful getting a judgment requiring the client to pay the money, I would have little hope of ever actually getting it.

Having this money in reserve makes the relationship with the client one of future money, not current. I have the freedom to terminate at will if the client is not complying with my policies. I have the ability to refuse constant schedule changes and not to tolerate any misbehavior. I have time to be picky when filling their child's slots.

I always let the state paid client know I have not billed for the three months when I reach that point in our relationship. I have them sign the required bi-weekly attendance sheets, but I do not turn in the billing. The client believes I am billing every other week until I mention I have not. By the three-month mark, the honeymoon is over in the daycare provider/parent relationship. By this time, a disagreement has occurred.

It is common for the state paid client to switch jobs within the first few months. The change of schedule almost always means longer hours and a more difficult work day. I only take state paid clients for specific time periods so a change in hours does not normally work out - especially if it means more direct care hours of the child. When the parent presents me with the schedule change, I reiterate that I will not take the funding for those hours. The parent believes I will do whatever it takes to keep their kid even if it means longer and more difficult hours. I tell them if they switch to this new job they will have to find different care. This sends a signal that I am willing to lose them if the parent cannot find work within the original hours I offered. When I make it clear their proposed changes will be accepted, the parent brings up the money and how I will lose two kids. This is when I tell them I have not made a dime off of their child because I have not billed for it. They are always very shocked to know I can live without their money.

This puts me on top of the change and sends the parent a clear message that I will not do just anything to have the money. The parent then has to decide if having their child with me is worth the extra effort to get another job with identical hours or try to keep the job they currently have. I am going to be okay either way. They are going to have to find a provider to take their kids immediately and in order to work the hours of the new job.

If a schedule change does not come up in the first three months, something else surely will. The parent either tries to pad the hours in care, bring their kid sick or for hours for which they are not funded or starts missing work. When problems arise, I address them immediately and set the boundaries of what I will tolerate. When the money comes up during a conflict, I drop the bomb that I have three months in reserve. I will not be held hostage by someone who thinks I will do whatever it takes to have the money. I do childcare to make a good living and I will not allow someone to threaten my income or happiness. Having three months in reserve for the state paid client buys me an insurance policy against their instability and misunderstanding of our roles.

Daycare Whispers...

Beware of scamming state paid clients. If you find out the parent is scamming the state, you may be obligated to report.

It is better to try to avoid being in the position of reporting fraud by screening your clients before enrollment. If the mom is not reporting the father is living with her and bringing income into the household, you may be obligated to report.

The state paid parent may be better off financially than you and your private pay customers.

Know your state's subsidy regulations regarding state paid parents bringing their children when they are not working or in school. If they are audited and have their child in care when they should not, the provider may have to repay the tuition. This is a common source of conflict between providers and state paid parents.

The closer the state paid client lives and works near your home, the better likelihood the relationship will last. A longer commute takes gas money and causes more wear and tear on the vehicle.

Consider taking sibling groups of state paid kids only if you can afford to lose them all at once. The mothers of sibling groups can become demanding because they understand they control a large portion of the provider's income.

The "My Child is Gifted" Parent

I have been wracking my brain in anticipation of writing this chapter, trying to figure out if there is anything more annoying than a parent who thinks their kid is gifted.

I am still thinking.

Childcare providers need a plan in place to deal with this phenomenon because it will come knocking at the door the first day the first parent comes to interview for the first slot. I do not know the exact statistics, but in my experience it seems that 98% of parents think their kid is gifted. Only 2% of kids actually are. You can go your whole career and never meet a truly gifted child. The number of parents who believe their kid is gifted is directly proportional to the number of parents who breathe.

My best gifted story: This really happened. I kid you not.

I interviewed a family who was expecting their second child. The first child was a preschooler. They lived nearby and were referred by someone who knew I did childcare. I could tell pretty early in the interview we did not have a match. The parents were both self-employed and the provider they would need would be one who works FOR them. This is a common parental want, but a service I do not provide.

They asked me to describe the curriculum I have for newborns. I responded that I am a care provider; I do not offer an educational program for infants. I do offer excellent food, friends, toys, exercise, supervision, deep, daily restorative sleep and love. I leave the education of the infants to their parents. I explained that despite not offering a curriculum and school, the kids who spend the first five years under our excellent care are all able to read, write and do simple math before they go to kindergarten. They are very sweet and kind and are a blessing to their Kindergarten teachers. I told them one of our graduates had just scored second in our district in a mathematics test and one had just completed testing for the gifted and talented program that she would be starting in the fall.

They told me that their preschool child was gifted. As my eyes began to roll so far up inside my head that I could not see forward, they followed with the proclamation that BOTH of them are gifted and their baby WOULD be gifted. They were the grand slam of giftedness. They were proclaiming the unborn baby gifted and that gifted newborn would need a gifted baby curriculum.

I tried. I really did. I started laughing and could NOT stop. I knew it was unprofessional, but a person can only take so much. I wanted to say, "excuse me, I need to get on the internet right now," and go post this on daycare.com so all my buddies could know I have officially heard it all. It simply does not get any better than that. Needless to say, the interview ended immediately. That was an hour of my life I could never get back.

The parental belief that their child is gifted is not that big of a deal. They have their child's whole childhood to figure it out. We all look at our kids as amazing and capable. It is part of loving them and having hope they will turn out great. It becomes a problem in childcare when parents expect the provider to be a servant to the giftedness. The requests for "special special" because the child needs his giftedness acknowledged, admired and fed can cause a lot of conflict with the parent and a bunch of time and money to the business.

Early potty training is one of the first attempts a parent makes to engage a provider in participating in a gifted activity for a baby. The bragging rights given to a parent who pronounces their infant potty trained are highly coveted. The supervision to catch the baby's non-verbal behavior before they have to eliminate requires a full-time adult. It is very time consuming to put an infant on a potty or hang them over a sink so they can go potty. The main problem for childcare is that it is extremely expensive in staff and cleaning time to take care of all the accidents. It ruins equipment. Refusal to participate can easily sever a childcare relationship.

Agreeing to participate can cost more than the provider makes a week on the child.

Another common belief is that the infant who crawls, pulls up and walks early is a gifted athlete. I had one family who insisted that their eight-month old stay awake all day and just do a few very short cat naps so he could be on the floor crawling, climbing and pulling up. I do two naps a day totaling four hours. I was not going to entertain having a frenetic infant up running my house so he could prepare for the 2020 games. They insisted the dad, a weekend softball player/weekday warehouse worker, was a superior athlete and the son was destined to be the same.

I have had a few parents tell me their child was gifted because he could watch television for hours at a time and not be distracted. I have had some tell me their two-month old was advanced because she could eat baby food. I had a mother a couple years ago pronounce genius on a one-year old who could operate her phone.

When a parent has a child that actually develops early or on the early end of the spectrum, they get a lot of attention. They post videos on YouTube and Facebook and use the word "genius" or "gifted" in the title. They get used to other adults praising them and being enamored by the child's early prowess. This only lasts until the child's age mates catch up. The parent does not get attention for the child walking early at eight months when the child turns thirteen months old and all the other thirteen month old toddlers are walking. That parent starts searching for other skills that will bring them the same praise and adoration. They do not want a one hit wonder.

The average parent believes the evidence that their child is gifted is, first and foremost, in reading. Writing and math come in as second and third. A parent may believe their child is ready to read if the child can recognize the letters of the alphabet and sing the ABC song. Recognizing the letter and number symbols is not an indicator that the child is ready to learn to read, but the parent wants daily proof that the child is being "worked with" on reading, math and writing. Often the parent practices the ABCs with the child, but stops there because it becomes hard work to get a child to recognize sounds and put letters together to make words. The parent turfs over all academic responsibility at the point where it becomes hard. It is hard because two and three-year olds are not ready to read.

The parent starts to engage the provider by asking for resources. They frame the discussion as needing help to solve a problem. The discussion goes like this: "Susie's is only sixteen months old and her vocabulary is that of a three year old. She can recite the alphabet, count to five in English AND Spanish, knows the name of the animals and what they "say". She can name twenty musical instruments, knows colors and has memorized all her favorite books. The problem I am having is in keeping her stimulated and finding new things she can learn. She's curious about EVERYTHING, but if you tell her something once she remembers it forever. It is that constant searching for something new that is so difficult for me as a parent. We do not have money to buy educational toys. We can barely afford to take her to the museum a few times a year. I play with her all the time. That is the majority of our day. We do lots of reading, some tablet time and playing. She's just a little SPONGE. Our goal is to get her in a gifted preschool, but we will have to get a scholarship because we cannot afford it."

That is the hook to get the provider to do something. The parent first says they need your opinion on resources for what they do with the child at home. Then the discussion goes to the questions about the resources you have in your childcare and what you will do. They have a problem and you can fix it. If you tell the parent that her description sounds like a normal sixteen-month old that has adults playing with them all day long, the parent becomes livid and insulted. If the provider wants the child enrolled, she has to play along and agree to become involved.

The parents may start demanding their child bring home worksheets, handwriting and crafts. Doing these activities with very small children between two and four years is very time consuming. Providers need to ask themselves if the three or four dollars an hour they receive for the care and supervision of the kids actually pays them to do this hard work. It is not enough for me.

If the provider does do academic work before the age of four and the child shows skills the parents can use to prove their child is gifted, it can actually backfire on the provider. The parent may decide the child is gifted and needs to go to a real school with real teachers. A plain ole daycare provider is not capable of educating their genius. Some parents will stay with a provider who is devoting a lot of her resources to early reading, math and writing, but many, if not most, will see the success the provider has with the child and want the child in a brick and mortar building with a principal and classrooms.

It is very common for parents to hire a provider who advertises a full academic program and still end up pulling the kid when they are three or four. If the provider would have known the parents were going to skip out the last year or so before kindergarten, they would not have done the HARD work it took to do academics with a child who was inherently too young. Waiting until they are four to begin pre-reading, pre-math and handwriting makes the adult's job way easier. The provider feels cheated that she invested so many resources into the child and now the child is going to a center or preschool during the years the provider really needs older children in her business to balance her state-mandated numbers.

(There is a way to solve this common phenomenon that I will delve into in a future part of the Daycare Whisperer Doing Daycare series. I have a system for avoiding the high cost of educating the very young and retaining the four and five-year olds in your business.)

It is very taxing on a home provider to work with parents who feel their child is very advanced or gifted when, in reality, the child is normal, below average or pervasively developmentally delayed. Parents will fixate on skill sets with their children that are quite normal, but the parent wants to believe they are indications that the child is advanced. In this day and age it is a slap to a parent's face to tell them the child is normal. The parent seeks a lot of discussion and action to address the child's advanced skills. When they are told that the child is perfectly normal and the provider has seen this many times, the parent is offended. There is little money in normal these days.

When the child is delayed or pervasively delayed it becomes astronomically harder to address issues. The parent believes the child is extremely smart and they do not want to hear that the child is displaying behaviors and skill sets requiring specific assessment and services. The only service the parent will readily agree to will be speech services because delayed speech is not associated with giftedness. Einstein did not speak until he was four. However, if speech is normal or advanced, it is also associated with giftedness in the parent's minds.

If the parent believes the child is highly intelligent and the provider believes the child is markedly delayed you do not have a single fleck of common soil to stand on together. The parent perceives the provider's assessment to mean the provider does not like the child or just does not know what she is talking about. Very often the phrase, "he does not do that at home," becomes the parent's way to stop the discussion. This is a capture trap phrase that translates to how the provider deals with and cares for the child, not an issue with the child.

When I know for certain the parent is exaggerating a child's skill set, I ask for a video. When the parent says the kid talks in paragraphs at home and I have not seen heard three words put together, I ask the parent to video the kid on their phone to show me. If the parent says the kid can read when they are not able to identify letters, I ask for a video. If a parent says the child is able to walk by themselves and I suspect they are exaggerating, I ask for a video. Cell phone video has made it possible for me to show parents what a child does in my house and for them to show me what the child does at home. The parent often drops the discussion when asked for video proof.

When the parent believes a child is advanced and starts to get wind that he is actually delayed, there is a stage-of-loss cycle that begins. Very often the parent just ignores it. They allow the child to go into Kindergarten without early intervention services despite being offered the resources that would clarify and provide services for the child's needs.

When providers sense the parent is getting angry when she is bringing up developmental and behavioral issues, often the provider backs off because she needs the money. If she presses too hard the parents will pull the child out of her daycare. She must endure story after story at her front door listening to how intelligent the child is and has to come up with just the right words to appease the parent, but not declare she agrees with the parent's assessment. When the parent senses the provider is not a believer, they escalate the gifted at home stories. It is exhausting to be put in a position where you have to witness the parent's fantasy and walk the tightrope of saying the right thing to keep the enrollment.

The provider knows that once the child goes to public school, free school, the big pond, the great equalizer, the parent will not be allowed to continue living in a fantasy. Once the child is in care where there is no money exchanged, the truth floats to the surface. The parent defends their current thinking until they start to see a whole class of their child's age mates. By the first conference, the parent goes from the child is gifted to he's "normal." By the second semester they see such a chasm that they are ready to accept assistance. It is unfortunate that the early intervention years were missed, but some parents will not step off of their dream of having a genius until the pedestal is knocked out from underneath them.

Some parents will eventually get to the acceptance stage of loss and will allow assessments and intervention. There is a segment of the parent population secretly wishing for a diagnosis like on the spectrum of autism or ADD to explain their child's behavior or delay. It is almost fashionable now to have a kid diagnosed on the spectrum because it implies the child is devoid in some areas but gifted in others. Partly gifted is better than not gifted at all.

There is a chance a provider who is working for many years may run across a truly gifted child. I have had two in my career. The funny thing was that both parents did not believe me when I started to see things in their child I hadn't seen before. I cautiously started talking to the parents about the possibility that they may have a little genius, but they shook it off and thought I was a little too bewitched by their kid. You cannot win in the game of gifted.

I was right on both counts. When they entered school they were invited into the gifted program. I was so fortunate to have those two full-time and get a glimpse into the mind of a baby genius. It was a blast watching them devour complex things and then switch to normal kid play. When you are in the same career for decades it is very exciting to see something new and then watch how it plays out.

Their parents were humbled by their child's intelligence and proceeded with mindful consideration. They wanted a well-balanced human being first. Giftedness is a gift, not an entitlement.

I have little tolerance for the "my child is gifted" parent. I have the vantage point of decades of experience and know the spectrum of parenting life. I am a parent myself. Our kids do not have to be the top of the heap to be valuable to us. It is okay for them to be average. It is discouraging to see how upset parents get when they are told their child is perfectly normal.

I have a friend with a preteen daughter who attended my childcare from birth to five. The daughter had her first seizure at my house when she was four. The child has a very serious life threatening form of epilepsy and has gone into cardiac arrest twice. She is on very powerful medication that dramatically affects her brain, body and academic abilities. She struggles in school and has to have incessant medical and academic intervention. What her mother would give to sit across a desk from a teacher at conference time and hear the words "she is perfectly normal." She never gets to hear those words or enjoy the relief that comes with them. She has to fight - and fight hard - for every specialist appointment to get medical and academic services. She has to devote her motherhood to this child's needs. She will never have a time in her life where this child will be able to be completely independent.

The parents who have normal kids and kids with needs that can be serviced are SO lucky and blessed. They need to get a grip and stop putting their parenting into something that is untrue and unnecessary. Parenting is not a contest and should not be a way to get attention from your friends and family. It is not an eighteen-year ego trip.

Since we all cannot have the top two percent children in intelligence, I would rather see us have value in giftedness that IS possible for every normal kid out there. I want our nation's parents to focus on early childhood giftedness in healthy eating, self-entertainment, deep, regular sleep, exercise, patience, self-restraint, empathy, kindness, following directions, hard work and respect for their elders. I will gladly participate in this kind of gifted early childhood education.

Daycare Whispers...

Do not engage in early potty training because a parent wants bragging rights. If you want the experience then go for it, but if not, say no.

If you have a child with what appear to be delays, your best bet to get him services is through a speech evaluation.

Do not participate in early baby food and table food introduction because the parent wants this type of gifted to brag about. Follow your normal routine.

Do not get sucked into doing a bunch of worksheets and flashcards for the early preschoolers because the parent believes the child needs them. Have them do it at home.

Get used to the gifted child syndrome. If you do not accept these parents, you will have an empty house every day.

The Permissive Parent

Permissiveness in child rearing knows no socioeconomic bounds. I have cared for children of all classes – from billionaires to the desperately poor living in abject poverty. The parents all look and act the same. Fortune 500 children have more stuff and a bigger place to live but their interactions with adults and other children are identical to the poorest children living in nearly empty public housing apartments.

A permissive parent chooses to raise their child without limits. They do not afford them the luxury of "no." They make little, if any, demands on their children and have few expectations of self-control. They relish in the comfort that their child who is selfish, aggressive and disrespectful of the rights of others is "normal." They do not assume responsibility because they are comfortable with their assessment that they are raising a naturally behaving child.

These parents are often kind, warm and loving parents. They offer deep respect for their own. They do not transfer that warmth and affection to their child's provider. The provider is being paid to have her rights trampled. The provider's children and daycare children are expected to be bystanders at best, and champions at most, of the child's CEO position in the childcare home.

This parent is not a parental attention seeking (PASS) parent. They could not care less what the provider thinks of them or their parenting. They are not allowing their child to do as they please, whenever they please, as a way to flip the middle finger to society. Rather, they are raising their children to live without limitations because they will not do the work of establishing boundaries and supervising the child within the confines.

Behavioral control is a requirement for a child to become integrated into the family and society and to ensure the child behaves with age appropriate maturity. Supervision, consistent disciplinary efforts and a willingness to take the child on if they do not comply are the essential tasks of behavioral control. The permissive parent refuses to exert any behavioral control. Short of immediate responses that rescue the child from immediate harm, the parent does not consider interceding to mold or direct their child's behavior.

The permissive parent is completely non-confrontational with their child but has no problem being confrontational with the provider. If the provider insists upon conferencing with the parent regarding the child's poor performance in care, the parent becomes angry with the provider and targets her tone, words or actions while she is explaining the issue. When the parent gets home and hears the child's story, the parent will call the provider and complain about how the provider behaved while disciplining the child or what another child did to provoke their child.

This becomes a huge liability as the parent accuses the provider of talking too sternly, holding the child's arm too tight when taking her to time out, keeping the child segregated for a long time or refusing to accept the child's apology. The parent deals with the entire incident with a singular interest in the provider and other children's behavior, not the act the child committed to receive a consequence.

This parent and their child behave terribly at drop-off and pick-up. If the child destroys the provider's property on the way into or out of the house, the parent does nothing. If the provider gives specific expectations to the parents regarding how the children are to behave on her property, the permissive parent will allow the child to directly disobey those rules.

I have heard countless stories of providers having rules that require children to stay out of their gardens, statues, front porches and bird feeders and have parents completely disregard the policy because their child wanted to pick flowers, throw rocks, dismantle bird feeders, hang off front porches, climb snow banks, etc. They are brazen enough to brag to the provider that their child wanted to have the flower or throw the rock so they allowed it in order to get the child in the door.

I spoke to one provider who told me a story of how the kids were destroying her newly planted flower garden. She told the parents that the children were not to pick her flowers or walk on the railroad ties bordering the garden. She sent a note home to each family that included the new rules. The very next day one of her four-year olds came running into the house with a demonic smile holding a flower she had picked. The mom proudly said, "look what Pookie picked for you, Ms. M!!!" The child said, "My mommy told me I could pick it for you, but I want Mommy to take it home." The mother just smiled, took the flower from the child's hand and told her she would keep it safe until she picked up the child later that day.

This parent is very dangerous to the provider because the permissiveness can lead to a child being injured or killed on or near her property. The parent allows a wide breadth of behavior on the daycare property, the adjoining neighbor's property and the street. It is not uncommon for it to take ten to twenty minutes for the parent to get their child into or out of the car. The child will lock the parent out of the car and climb around in the front seat playing with the steering wheel and brakes.

The permissively parented child will be extremely violent with the parent. They will begin being violent as infants and it will escalate to serious levels as they get to the age of four and five when they can cause damage to the adult. They will also fight like a caged animal when they are disciplined by the provider. The parent will do absolutely nothing when told about their child's behavior.

The parent allows the child to behave like a baby long past infancy. They use baby talk and carry the child when the child has been walking for years. They spend a long time at the door tickling, singing and loving up their child as they would a newborn baby. They often have older preschoolers who have a pacifier all day, a blanket to carry around, sippy cups or bottles to drink from and as many items from home as the child wants. They completely disregard any direct policy prohibiting items from home. They will allow the child to smuggle in small items such as coins, cars and toys. They will insist the child must have large items like pillows, couch cushions and comforters.

If the child has an older, school-aged sibling, the parent will pick up the sibling first and bring the sibling into the daycare when she picks up her child. She wants the older child to run rampant in the house and have some fun with the younger sibling. Even with directions to keep the older child at the front door, the parent allows him to go into the playroom and any other area he wishes. The parent cannot trust the school-aged child to behave in the car while the younger child is being picked up so they talk the child into coming into the provider's house by telling them they can play for a bit.

The parent is much more comfortable taking on the provider and her policies than telling the child no. The only time they show an iota of remorse for the provider's unhappiness in dealing with their child is the day they are given notice that the child can no longer attend. They need childcare the next day so they play nice and finally commit to talk to their child. They are secretly fuming because they truly believe it is the provider's job to make the same allowances for the child. They begin to search for other childcare immediately and often terminate the childcare before the notice time the provider gave. A phone call to the State is made in retaliation of the termination.

The permissive parent is blindsided when society demands they deal with the child. They feel they have given their child so much love and attention that the child will naturally turn out well. They believe love and attention are ALL the child needs. By the time they find out rules, boundaries and expectations are as important as love, it is too late. Unless the child miraculously ends up in a very strict authoritative school system, they have little hope of becoming a contributing member of society.

Daycare Whispers…

The permissive parent does not care what the provider thinks of their parenting.

The parent is much more comfortable taking the provider and her policies on than telling the child no.

The permissive parent is non-confrontational with their child but has no problem being confrontational with the provider.

The walk from the car to the house and the house to the car is a very high liability period for the provider. Supervise the parent and child and be firm that the child must obey the rules on your land.

This parent is very dangerous to the provider because the permissiveness can lead to a child being injured or killed on or near her property.

Do not allow older, non-enrolled siblings to come into the daycare when picking up the younger child.

The "Hard Core Pawn" Parent

The Hard Core Pawn parent is fronting something that is not real. They fabricate, exaggerate and fixate on their own parental prowess and vast knowledge of their own child. Because they are the parent, they want the provider to agree with this and do as they are told without question. They are, simply put, a bully. They use their parental rights and status as a parent to force the provider to do what they want and to respect them at a level they have not earned.

The Hard Core Pawn parent makes their superior parenting expectations their primary form of communicating with the provider. They have the time and the energy to keep up a high level of interaction. They may not work fulltime or they have jobs with low expectations so they do not have much to manage other than their baby. They are not the boss in public, but they are the boss with their spouse and, quite possibly, their own parents. They look at the childcare relationship as an extension of their family boss role.

The frustrating part of dealing with these parents is that even when things are going really well, they will not accept it. They want to micromanage every little detail of their child's life and want to conference and lay down the law about their perception of anything not perfect for their little Pookie. If there is nothing going on, they will invent it. They will make accusations that cannot be proven or denied and expect the provider to do something about it. They will say things like "she had too much sun in her eyes when she was outside" or "the color yellow makes her sad."

This is extremely hard to manage when dealing with a first-time parent. They do not know very much about childcare, so how they interpret every breath the Pook takes is often incorrect. What they attribute the problem to be, whether real or imagined, and how they solve it, is often developmentally inappropriate, unnecessary and unmanageable. Their end game solutions are almost always rooted in one-to-one care of the child and total engagement of themselves until they declare the issue invalid or resolved. The typical provider copes with this parent by very carefully choosing ANY concern she shares about the child. She knows the turmoil that will come her way if she suggests there is anything wrong. She knows she cannot even give a simple suggestion of something to do with Pookie that will not land her in hours of conferencing and text messaging. If she brings up anything other than black-and-white, provable medical information, she is going to pay in spades for engaging the parent.

This parent commands attention by turning any normal thing the baby into a crisis. They dramatically overreact to crying. If their child is crying, the adult caring for them MUST be doing something wrong, is inept and must be trained. They place blame on the methods the provider is using and want to dictate how it should be done differently so their child does not cry. They use the phrase, "she never does this at home" daily. They hyper-focus on any illness or minor skin irritation their child has. They question every pimple, booger and goober on the kid's body. They get overly upset if the child is not perfectly clean when they pick them up and make dramatic gestures, both physically and verbally, as they clean the child in front of the provider. They do not run off to the doctor every time the kid farts. They are not Munchausen by Proxy parents. They do not want an authoritarian, such as a doctor, in the middle of their perceptions. They are one of the most challenging parents to get to seek medical care when the child is ill because they know more than the doctor does.

When they fabricate concerns, they know there is not really anything wrong, but they thrive on any opportunity to be the boss. They will suck the life out of a provider in parent conferencing, blow up her phone with questions on her time off and come to the worst possible conclusion to every minor concern. This goal is to make the provider feel incompetent and the parent to appear to be the expert. They demand attention and respect be given to the All Powerful, All Knowing, Parent Wizard behind the Curtain.

The Hard Core Pawn parent looks a lot like the picky parent when you first start interviewing the family, but they are not the same. The picky parent is one who wants to dictate what goes on with their baby when they are away. The picky parent may have good intentions and often settles down once they see the child is coming home in great condition every day. This parent also gets bored with the pickiness over time. It is easy to be exact with a baby when the baby is the only thing you have to do.

When the picky parent returns to work they have a lot more on their mind. They have a tendency to gradually triage their life and the miniscule details of their baby's life in childcare become pretty low on their priority list. They have a wrecked house, a ton of laundry, a boss who wants them back to full capacity and a baby who keeps them up at night. Their plate is too full to pick at everything on it. Their pickiness may surface now and then in waves, but they become less frequent and intense.

This parent also has characteristics of the PASS (Parental Attention Seeking Syndrome) parent but there is one key difference. This parent will force an immediate termination and it will be an ugly event that favors the provider with a nasty complaint and inspection. Since this parent insists on the last word, there is a very high likelihood a complaint of child abuse or neglect will be raised.

I call this parent the Hard Core Pawn parent as a shout out to one of my favorite reality shows. It is one of my guilty pleasure series I love watching when I need to have mindless entertainment. There is a little lesson in human behavior on this show in the formula they use to show the worst behaving customers.

The customer comes into the pawn shop with something to sell and they are very sweet with soft nonverbal behavior. They are interested in selling their great-great grandmother's 18-karat gold ring with incredibly rare diamonds and they want a ton of money for it. After the owner looks at the piece and informs the customer it is a worthless fake, the attack begins. The customer accuses them of not knowing jewelry and trying to rip them off. The owner asks, "How can I rip you off if I am not trying to buy it from you?"

The next step is for the customer to begin latching onto anything the owner says. Any words are turned into an accusation of being treated badly. No matter how polite the owner is the customer finds SOMETHING in the way they said it or how they looked when they said it. Instead of the discussion being about the actual piece of jewelry, it quickly turns into how the customer is being treated. It finally ends with the customer refusing to leave until they get their money and it turns violent as they are tossed out the door like a ragdoll by a six-foot five, four-hundred pound security guard.

This is the same cycle as the Hard Core Pawn parent in childcare. It ends in an immediate termination because these badly behaving daycare parents are trying to hock something that is not real.

The Hard Core Pawn parent requires the provider to believe that they know best, even though their expertise exists only in their own mind. They demand the utmost respect for their, "I know my baby best and I know what's best for my baby," mantra. They command that respect by insisting that only THEY know how to care for the child and they are there to make sure you do it their way. Their idea that they are the boss of the provider is not real. They do not trust anyone to care for their child so if the provider is going to be honored to have their little Pookie, she will pay an extremely high price as she jumps through their hoops of daily suspicion and interrogation and immediately offers up a promise of compliance.

Inevitably, the newbie parent will come across an experienced, worn out caregiver who refuses to comply and give respect where it hasn't been earned. The parent will be told their precious ring is a fake and the provider is not going to pay for it anymore. The second this happens, the Hard Core Pawn parent senses they are being dethroned and lashes out. Instead of discussing the disagreement of care, they focus not on what the provider did but what she said and what she looked like saying it. ANYTHING that happens during the initial wave of anger when they are being dismissed will become the issue at hand. This parent wants the provider back to the state of worship, adoration, respect and compliance.

When they are told the provider is done, they can get very nasty. They do not care who is in the childcare. They will yell, cuss and threaten the provider in front of kids, staff and incoming parents. The best thing for the provider to do is to terminate the parent over the phone and make arrangements for the child's belongings to be off property when they are picked up. The provider does not have the back up of a four-hundred pound bouncer. If she is alone with the children she can put herself and the kids in danger. The key is to know when enough is enough and get the parent out the door with as little conflict as possible.

The best defense is a good offense. With experience, the provider will be able to pick out some of these parents during the interview process. Sometimes people do not show their true colors until a few weeks into the relationship, so these parents can slip through the cracks. The one marker I have seen for this type of parent is the dad who does a disproportionate amount of care for the newborn baby. During the interview, the dad will control the dialogue and talk incessantly about how he gets up in the middle of the night and does all the diaper changes. He acts like he gets a lot of attention and praise from family and friends for being such an involved dad. He pauses when he describes his care of the child in anticipation of the provider to congratulate and praise him. Now, not every dad who is involved with their newborn is a Hard Core Pawn parent. The difference is shown in the bragging as opposed to the acknowledgement that it is hard to care for a newborn in the first few weeks and the dad is a team player. If the mom sits sheepishly quiet during the dad's proclamation of his prowess as a parent, beware. If the mom smiles, nods her head and looks relieved, you have a great chance of having a terrific daddy to work with.

Daycare Whispers...

Do not allow a parent to present themselves as the expert on their child. They are a parent and have only singular knowledge of their own child. They definitely do not know their child as a group care member. Their opinion is important to listen to, but it cannot turn into demands that exceed the service agreement.

When the parent is fixating on inconsequential issues with the child, shut them down immediately. Be cheery and say "no" to it becoming a crisis in the parent's mind.

Become the "alpha dog" in the relationship.

If you allow this parent to get to the point where they revel in their authority over you and instill fear in you with their every appearance, be prepared for the final straw to explode like fireworks. It is going to get ugly. Terminate them over the phone, not in person.

Single Moms

I have had the pleasure to be the provider to children being raised by single moms. I have seen women who were forced into single parenting by an absent father and rise like a phoenix to take on the task and do it very well. I have had a few single dads and each one of them was a stellar client.

The care of a child who is parented by one parent is a little different than a child from a married family. The schedule is often the biggest issue because the hours the child is in care cannot be shortened by having the parent who goes into work last drop-off and the parent who gets off first pick-up.

Other than the flexibility of shorter care hours, I have not seen much difference in the children of single parents compared to married parents. Sometimes it is actually easier to only have one parent to keep happy. Single dads are notoriously easy to keep happy. Most providers I know really enjoy working with them.

I started home childcare in the early nineties when the entitlements for single parents were dramatically less in cash value compare to what is available today. Today, the term "Single Mom" has become synonymous with concession in our society. It is a term that embodies a struggling person to whom we should bestow charity and understanding. We equate raising a child without a father as something we should compensate for by providing for the mom and child in order to balance out their disadvantage.

When the single mom comes to the daycare table she has had a history of receiving because she is the only parenting parent. If she is poor or in a low paying job she is offered assistance such as food, health insurance, housing, and childcare. If she makes too much to qualify for assistance she may ask for concessions because she does not qualify.

I am a single mom. I have been for fourteen years. The idea of being given any benefit that would balance out my family's financial life because my son does not have a father never occurred to me until I kept reading posts on daycare boards such as daycare.com and the childcare section of Craigslist. The providers on daycare.com told stories of single moms requesting special pricing and schedules because they were single. They were encountering moms who asked for a "single mother discount" on the first phone contact.

The single moms on Craigslist advertise they need long or odd hours because they are single parents. Sometimes they ask for the provider to offer diapers and formula. There is no shame in the single mom game. It is perfectly acceptable now to ask for others to offer goods and services for free or nearly free based solely upon being a single parent.

When I am called and asked for a single mom discount I answer them with a question. "What are you doing to help other single moms?" If the mother believes single mothers need a hand up and a hand out then she would be the first to offer that. She may not have money, but she has the same 24 hours in a day I do. I ask her if she is providing childcare on her non-working hours to other single moms who cannot afford care. If she works forty hours a week, she still has at least 120 hours a week for single mom community service. If she uses her evenings and weekends to help out other women in her position then I am more than willing to help her out. I am a single mom, too.

When my brother and I were young, our mom was a single mom. She had two single girlfriends she had known since junior high and between the three of them, they had seven kids within five years of each other. There was no such thing as childcare assistance in the sixties so they had to rely on each other for help. While they were working the seven of us went from one mom to another. One mom worked days, one worked evenings and one worked overnight. Between the three of them they covered each other's childcare needs for years. The seven of us were together a lot. Life was easier on these single mothers during the school year, but when summer came around they simply planned their work schedules around each other's jobs and they made it work. They did not have to pay each other or leave their kids with strangers.

The idea of childcare sharing went out of societal consciousness when the government stepped in and offered free childcare to low-income parents. There are no expectations that the single mother will make a Herculean attempt to work it out on her own before going to the taxpayers for help. Single mothers with one child, making $12/hour wages are the ones who do not qualify for this assistance. Consequently, they are often the ones asking total strangers to discount services based on their single mother status.

When asked, there hasn't been a single mother asking for a discount able to answer what she is doing to help other single moms. When I talk further with them about it they get angry. They do not want to spend their time off with other people's kids. They want time with their own child on their time off and they need time to rest on the weekends. I understand this, but if they are not willing to provide for others what they are asking for themselves, then they truly do not believe single mothers need the help. Put your time where your mouth is, then my mouth will say, "Yes."

There is an expectation of daycare providers to be volunteers or, at the least, give concessions to help out the unfortunate single mothers with their children. Other vendors of child-related goods or services do not offer free or discounts based on the parent only having one income. McDonald's does not have a separate menu for single moms. Wal-Mart does not have a ten percent discount at the register for their single mom customers. Gymboree does not have a single mom blue dot special.

Instead of offering free or near free, it is time to empower single moms to take their place in our nation's economy and start to give instead of take. Nearly forty percent the children in the US under the age of five are living with a single mother. The percentage increases every decade. It is time for single moms to band together and lead our nation in helping each other out. We single moms will soon become the majority and with that comes responsibility, not liability.

I encourage providers to think about whether or not they want to choose single mothers as their offering of community service. If you do, please ask first what the single mom does for others in her position. As John F Kennedy once said, "Ask not what your country can do for you, ask what you can do for your country."

Daycare Whispers...

If you decide to discount the price of childcare for single moms do it because this is the community service you want to offer. Do not do it because it is expected for you to give and them to receive.

Consider asking the single mom what she is doing to assist other single moms. She may be able to get other single moms to pick up early so the child's daycare day is shorter.

When something is given for free it often has little value to the recipient. You may believe it is valuable, but the recipient may only believe it is valuable the day they receive the news they will receive it. After that, it is considered owed as opposed to an ongoing benefit.

Be prepared to deal with the possibility that the single parent receiving a myriad of free subsidies is actually better off financially than you and your private pay customers.

The UnParent

There are parents who only want to care for their children when they are sleeping. It is easier for them to be parents if all they have to do is get the child out of bed, put him in the car seat, drive to childcare, pick them up from childcare, drive home from childcare, do a quick supper and bath and put the child to bed.

This style of parenting is quite common with parents of children who attend daycare centers. When infants and toddlers go to centers, they get a very small amount of sleep during the day. The rooms are very noisy and the florescent lights are always on. By the time the baby and one-year old leave daycare, they are exhausted and often fall asleep in the car seat on the way home. The parent gets used to being able to take the child home in the early evening and put them in bed within an hour. The child passes out and sleeps a long eleven to twelve-hour night, which gives the parent a substantial amount of time to themselves in the evening. Although they have their child on the weekends, they typically spend a large amount of their family time running around in the car where the child is buckled in a carseat. Weekends are also prime time for grandparent visits and overnights.

As the child ages, the amount of time they can stay awake after daycare increases. Unfortunately, the parent is unprepared for this change. They have had a long haul of easy and early bedtime so when the child is awake longer, the time they had reserved for their relaxation and "me" time is decreased.

When the child nears the age of two they are usually in a sleeping room in childcare away from infants. This leads to a better and longer nap. Once the child starts having a solid afternoon nap they will not go to bed an hour after getting home. This is a common time for parents to start requesting a longer daycare day. They want to drop off earlier and pick up closer to when the center closes even though their work hours have not changed. They are not able to get the same things done around the home as they used to when the child was younger. They increase childcare hours so they can go home, get supper and laundry started and rest before the child gets home. They try to replicate the same amount of sleeping time they enjoyed when the child was a baby. Even with maximum hour usage in childcare, the child starts wanting to stay up past 7 p.m. at home. This is when the parent starts asking the childcare to decrease the afternoon nap and get the child up earlier in the afternoon in order to maintain an early bedtime. This request quickly escalates to requesting the child not nap at all.

This parent commonly brings the child to childcare in the morning and returns home to get ready for work. If the child sleeps while the parent is getting ready they will leave him sleeping, but if he wakes up and cries the parent gets him out of bed and takes him straight to daycare. The child is not fed before childcare because the parent has learned that if they feed them in the morning, they have to change diapers and possibly even change clothes if the child spits up. Most babies will have a bowel movement and soak through an already saturated night diaper if they are fed right when they wake up. It is easier for the parent to just listen to the fussing on the way over to childcare and hand the child off in their pajamas and night diaper with an empty belly. The childcare provider will clean, change, dress and feed the child.

Home childcare has a different cycle. Most home providers have a quiet separated area where the infant can sleep and require both a morning and afternoon nap. The home care child goes home much more rested and is not ready for bed an hour after arrival. Parents who do not want to deal with alert children will start complaining that the child is up too late at night and will begin quizzing the provider about sleep times. They want to cut the morning nap out and have the provider just do one nap. They request the nap to be from 11 a.m. to 1 p.m. The parent knows from their experience with the baby on the weekends that if this schedule is followed, the baby will go to sleep easily by 6-7 p.m. since they will be awake for five to six hours straight in the afternoon.

It would be a rare home provider that would allow a schedule such as this because she wants a full afternoon break that ends closer to the time when the kids begin departing. The average home provider ends nap around 3 p.m. Having a toddler or infant awake for two hours during nap so a parent does not have to deal with the child from 7-9 p.m. is not acceptable to most home providers. Consequently, this parent will often switch to a center to have the shorter, earlier naps and the longer days. Most centers have a flat fee and allow the parents to bring the child from open to close for the same price. The typical center is open twelve hours a day.

I had a consulting contract in 2011 watching cameras and doing health and safety consultations for a daycare center. I was able to watch the cameras from my home, turning them on around 5:30 a.m. and turning off when the center closed around 6:00 p.m. The twelve-hour children were about ten percent of the population of the two centers. I could tell the parents who were on twelve-hour days because they were the only parents in the building at both open and close, five days a week. They arrived in yoga pants with their hair askew in the morning and returned in the evening dressed in suit and ties and dresses. I knew they were the same babies and toddlers because of the car seats and the outerwear on the kids.

The external center cameras showed these parents sitting out in the parking lot before the doors were opened in the morning. They would also sit in their car and wait until the minute before closing time to come to the door to get the child when the center closed. They were a bit of a handful for the workers because they would want to do conferencing about their child right at the minute the center was closing, forcing the workers to remain in the room when they were anxious to go home.

These parents are very upfront about preferring the childcare doing the awake time and them doing the sleep time care of their child. They feel they are better parents and spouses if they have time to themselves every day. They often are good financial clients and are generous with their providers with gifts and cards. They are very grateful when the provider is willing to have the child during all but one of the waking hours of the day. They are excellent about bringing supplies and spare clothes and they provide nice clothing for the provider to put on the child.

They will sometimes ask for the provider to dress the child in their pajamas before leaving care. They will often ask the provider to give supper to the child as most childcares do lunch around eleven. It is a long haul without a meal from 11-6 p.m. so the toddler and preschooler are starving by the time the parent gets them home. If the childcare provides supper, then only baths and a snack consume the hour of parent time before the child is put to bed.

These parents seek out providers who have long open hours for a flat fee. This is often found in new providers who are willing to take any schedule to get clients. If the provider requests the parents to limit the hours of care to just their work and transport times, the parents willingly leave the childcare and seek out either an open hour center or another home childcare willing to do the full twelve hours. The full 12-hour day and the willingness to have the child up the entire nap are the two services these parents look for when interviewing.

These parents become very upset when the child is excluded for illnesses and are one of the biggest offenders of the dope-and-drop. They will bring their child out in any inclement weather to bring the child to care. Even if their area is in a state of emergency, come hell or high water they will make it to daycare. If they are told their child is the only child attending care because the other parents would not risk taking their kids out on bad roads, the parent is thrilled because their Pookie gets to have the provider to themselves that day. One to one time with an adult is highly prized - as long as the parent is not that adult.

They often look for providers close to home so they can be assured they can get their child to care despite snow and road closings. If they cannot shovel their car out of the driveway they will carry them or bring them by stroller. They make arrangements for the child to be in another childcare or with relatives when the provider is on vacation. The parents take vacations without their child and often ask the provider if she is willing to keep the child around the clock during the time they are out of town on vacation. It is usually workable for the provider to have the child while the parents are on vacation because the only thing they have to do in addition to their regular daycare day is feed supper, bathe and put the child to bed. It is pretty easy money.

It is very common for these parents to try for another baby when their firstborn is nearing the age of two. When the mother is off on maternity leave, the firstborn attends daycare full time. The newborn second child often enters care before maternity leave ends in order for the mother to have a break before returning to work.

The way to avoid having unparents in your childcare is to limit the total number of hours a child can attend daily. I cap my hours at nine hours per day. I specifically look for clients who have the parent who goes into work last do the drop off and the parent who gets off of work first do the pick-up. If the parent is a single parent or one parent does both drop-off and pick-up, I only interview the ones who have a half hour lunch, fifteen-minute transport time to work and an eight-hour day work day. If the parent states they have to do overtime I do not interview them unless they can make arrangements for someone else to pick up the child at the normal time.

Another method of ensuring the parents are parenting is to not feed babies or older kids upon arrival. Expect every child to be fed before they come to daycare. I make what I call "second breakfast" at 8:30 a.m. If the kids arrive before meal time they have to be able to make it until second breakfast is served. I do not accept parent's claims of the child refusing to eat or of having eaten so early in the morning that they will need another bottle soon. I have it in my policies that I do not offer a bottle to babies until 9 a.m. which is when the older kids are done eating breakfast. The baby must be fed before coming to care. If the baby refuses to eat, the parents need to keep the baby home until she does. I also do not accept half eaten bottles. I will not finish a bottle because it quickly turns into a full feeding if I allow any feedings upon arrival. I do not allow parents to bring children in their night diapers or in their pajamas unless they can stay in their pajamas all day. I do not change clothes, brush teeth or do hair. The child must be completely ready for childcare every day when they arrive.

Lastly, do not allow parents to influence sleep schedules. I do not provide service to children who do not need a full afternoon nap. I do not shorten naps or rearrange them for one child. If the parents want a shorter, earlier or no nap service, they have to find other care arrangements. Keeping the children on a sleep rest schedule that works for the group and offers me a long quiet break every afternoon is what makes me happy and able to keep doing childcare year after year, decade after decade. It is about me and what I need to be happy in this job and is where the credit is due for my longevity in the business.

The daycare provider can choose what type of children and parents they want to work with. Personally, I want the parent to spend TIME with the child in the morning. Every kid deserves to have time with their parents before going out into the world. Requiring the parents change diapers, dress, feed and brush teeth every morning compels them to spend face-to-face awake time with their child.

I am not in the business of providing services that allow a parent to not parent. I do not want to work with that parent and I do not want their money. I really do not want the child who is being raised without parents. They have severe issues that escalate as they age. I cannot be their parent regardless of how much I love them and take great care of them. I am good, but I am not THAT good!

Daycare Whispers...

Do not set up your schedule to allow the parents to not parent in the evening.

Do not arrange or shorten the child's nap for the parents.

Do not allow parents to bring their children to daycare without preparing them for the day.

Do not allow parents to force you into not being the bearer of bad news. They do not get to hear only good things about their kid.

Cap your hours off to the total number of hours each child can attend. I cap mine at nine. This alone will be your biggest offense in preventing an unparenting parent from choosing you.

When unparents have their second child, it is going to get worse. Not having room for number two may be a way to easily get rid of number one.

The Parent Who Brings Children Dirty (i.e., Pigpen's Parents)

There are parents who simply do not care if their kid is clean. They bring them to daycare in a full night diaper and claim the child peed on the way. They bring them in soiled, poopy diapers with the same claim. Parents who do this believe they are the first parent to ever try to pass a fully loaded diaper off as a beyond-my-control event. All they have to say is, "it happened in the car," and they do not have to change their kid in the morning.

One of the most difficult discussions a provider will have with a parent is about children being brought to childcare dirty. It happens to all of us. The diplomatic provider wants a way to bring up the unclean child without offending the parent. We do not want to say the child is dirty and stinks. Most providers will try bringing up this issue in a casual, joking matter and follow with some understanding words about how kids will be kids, hoping the parent will take the hint. This approach never works and the provider becomes frustrated because a nice roundabout message went right on by the parent.

I have a friend who did childcare for her neighbor across the street. The dad had the kids from the time they woke up until eight in the morning. Every day he would walk across the street to the daycare with the baby still in her pajamas, sporting crusty hair, a dirty face and a soiled diaper. Every single day he would claim the baby would not let him dress her, comb her hair or wash her face. He said she pooped on the way across the street. What are the odds of a kid pooping at the exact same time, every single day on a mere fifty foot walk from one front door to another?

The truth is he gave the baby a bottle in bed when she awakened and left her in the crib until the minute the daycare opened. He did not do a single thing for the baby. He was able to come up with some words and get out of caring for his kid. My friend finally had enough and started having a changing pad ready at the door for when he arrived. She instructed the dad to either take the kid back home to get her ready for daycare or clean her up at the front door. A couple times of doing this and the dad started doing it at home before he trudged across the street. Miraculously, the baby changed her pooping schedule when he was no longer allowed to bring her dirty.

Parents do not realize that the provider knows the difference between a diaper that is freshly soiled and one that has remained on the child for hours. They know the difference in the smell, how dried to the skin it is and the sheer volume. Kids do not have giant, balloon bladders and cannot flood a diaper with stale urine in a fifteen minute car ride.

If the parent is wise to the fact that the provider knows he's lying, he does not care. If those words get him out of tending to his child, then those words are going to be used. When dealing with unclean children, you will see a pattern of parents using words to excuse themselves of their responsibility. "He's been playing outside all the time." "He would not let me cut his nails." "I just washed his clothes yesterday." "He will not let me wash his hair." "I changed him right before we left." "Boys will be boys." And, the ever popular, "Dad said he gave them a bath last night." The parents know that addressing this issue is an uncomfortable conversation for the provider to have. This is their assurance that they will not be called out for doing it. If the provider confronts the parents, it is often done so politely and superficially that the parent walks away from the conversation without an ultimatum that the kid MUST come clean.

Some providers will talk about this concern in their newsletter, hoping that by addressing many, they will get their point across to one. This never works. The parent who will not take the time to clean their kid is not going to take the time to read a newsletter. Even if they would happen to read it, they will not believe it is directed to them because previous conversations about their kid's cleanliness have always ended with an understanding that it happens. Kids get dirty. The parent wants to accept that understanding rather than bathe their kid.

There is only one way to deal with this parent: you have to tell them the truth and set exact expectations. You have to tell them that Johnny is dirty and give specifics: his ears are filthy, his fingernails are dirty, his feet are black, he smells like spoiled milk or cigarettes, his diaper area smells foul, his hair is unclean, he's been in the same clothes for three days, the garage sale clothes smell musty, etc. They need to understand that it is difficult for you to snuggle and hold a baby that is dirty and stinks. We want to be close to the children, but we will avoid physical contact if they are unclean. The best way to get a provider to spend a lot of time holding a baby is to have that baby clean and smelling delicious.

Once you tell them what the problem is, you give them the solution. I use the phrase, "he needs to come perfectly clean, every single day. His clothes must be freshly laundered and his body needs to be absolutely clean from head to toe."

This sounds like a scary conversation to have because the parent will be upset. However, they will not be upset that you said these words; they will be upset because they have to start keeping the kid clean. If you said, "Johnny is dirty and his diaper is full every day so I will give him a bath, brush his hair and teeth, wash his clothes and trim his nails," the parent would not mind being told the kid was dirty. They would be cool with the conversation if the end game was that you would do everything and they would do nothing.

Once you have laid down the law, you can offer to delve into why the child is dirty and has soiled clothes. There are some situations where the parent does not have access to inexpensive laundry. In this day and age, there should not be an issue with access to water, soap and shampoo. If the parent needs help getting toiletries, I would gladly supply them. If they do not have hot running water and a tub, I will allow them to bathe their kid at my house. I have done this before. It is a pain to bathe your kid at someone else's house and only the ones who truly needed it took me up on this offer. I have also taught parents how to hand wash and dry clothes. My grandparents did not have access to low-cost laundry services and they managed to wash clothes for themselves and ten children. Even if they do not have the luxury of a washer and dryer, parents still need to be responsible for keeping their kids clothes clean. If they have to wash by hand and line dry, then that is what they have to do.

Some providers try to avoid confronting parents by bathing the kid and washing the kid's clothes and outerwear. The ones who are nervous about bathing a child will use a pack of wet wipes and try to wipe them down. They hope the parent will notice they have done the work and be embarrassed by it, but this is never the outcome. The parent does not acknowledge the provider's help or how clean the kid is. They realize that the child and their clothes are clean, but it will not be mentioned because they are not embarrassed; in fact, they are happy. After all, the kid is clean and they do not have to give them a bath. And with clean clothes, well… they get to keep them on the kid another day or two. Their focus is not about what the provider has done, but rather, what they no longer have to do.

When parents send the kid dirty with filthy clothes and diapers, they are being lazy. Call it what you will, but 99.99% of the time, this is the root problem. Remember that our ancestors had to fetch water to boil on a stove heated by wood they chopped. That was hard work. Today's parents have hot running water, cheap soap and detergent, nail clippers and shampoo. It is not THAT hard to wash a baby or toddler. It is not hard to change a poopy diaper. It is easy to cut fingernails and to wash clothes. Any fool can do it. This is not the time to be making excuses for them. Expect them to do the right thing and refuse to care for the kid if they do not. Do not do it for them and do not be nice.

You should not expect to get support from human service agencies that serve childcare homes or resource and referral agencies that train childcare providers. The current school of thought for managing unclean children is to simply respect the parent's lifestyle choice. This includes their acceptance of their kid being dirty or infested with lice. I have spoken with many providers who are attending classes teaching this point of view. Some providers have called child protective about children who have severely unmet hygiene needs. Unfortunately, if the child does not have untreated sores or undeniable illness because of poor hygiene, the complaint may fall on deaf ears.

It is the parent's right to decide how clean they want the child to be. It is your option to terminate the care if you do not want to host their choice. I am not going to have dirty kids in my house and I am not going to allow the spread of head lice because a parent wants to exercise their parental rights under my roof. I do not care what the best practice is, nor do I care what the human services agencies think I need to tolerate. Unkempt children with nuisance diseases, such as lice, are not protected under the disability act and we are not obligated to serve them. I will gladly tell child protective I will not be a party to this lifestyle choice at the same time I tell the parents. I am willing to face whatever consequences come from this decision.

One lesson I have learned from over two decades of doing childcare is that the things most difficult to say are the things that need to be said the most specifically. If you are uncomfortable in the beating-around-the-bush conversations, you may as well just go for it and be uncomfortable in the direct-to-the-point conversations. It is better to get it over with and send the message that you are going to take them on if they do not do the right thing by the kid.

Remember, you are self-employed and you and your family have the right to be happy in your home. I do not know anyone who wants to be around unclean, stinky people. You should be able to work without being grossed out over a kid's musty clothes covered in food from three days ago. You should not have to hold the hand of a kid sporting a quarter inch of dirt in their fingernails. You do not have to have dirty feet on your couch and floors. You can (and should) demand that anyone who resides in your home for any portion of the day be bug-free, odor-free and clean.

Daycare Whispers...

Directly tell parents your expectations of cleanliness.

Do not bathe the child or do their laundry.

Use the phrase perfectly clean: "Susie needs to come perfectly clean every day."

Do not address many in order to reach one. Putting nice notes in newsletters or doorway signs will not work.

Do not allow children to come in overnight diapers and clothes.

Creeper Dad

Most dads have limited contact with the provider during the day and when they pick-up or drop-off they do it quickly. However, there are some dads who become infatuated with the childcare provider and use their kid in the daycare as a way to get the provider's attention.

One common trait of these dads is that they hang out for long periods at drop-off and pick-up. If they have the children in their care when the mom is at work, they try to stay at the provider's house for as long as the provider will allow. They do not respond to a single hint that it is time to leave. At drop-off, they make themselves at home pretending their child needs them to stay. At pick-up, they will go as far as to undress a child in winter gear and send them back into the playroom to continue playing so they can force the provider to spend time with them.

They enjoy sitting in the playroom and watching the provider work. They love the conversation she is forced to have with them out of politeness. They really love having someone else take care of their kid while providing the toys and space for free.

If the dad frequently calls and texts to check up on the child throughout the day, it is a red flag that he is using the child's well-being as a way to force an interaction with the provider. The dad will also purposely not pay the provider at the normal time so he has an excuse to come back to the daycare during off-hours.

If they are successful getting any attention, they begin to escalate the contact by saying small, inappropriate phrases like, "you smell good today" or "I like those jeans." Any change in the provider's appearance will bring about comments. If the provider changes her hair color it will be mentioned the second the dad sees it. He will comment on the change and then relate it to himself with a phrase like, "Oh, you colored your hair blonde. I like blondes." When left unchecked, the dad begins non-verbal as well as verbal advances. He will look directly at the provider's chest and say something like, "looking at you is a great way to start the day".

The provider senses the dad is behaving more than nice but brushes it because she does not want to lose the kid. The dad banks on this. It takes something more brazen to shake the provider into realizing the dad is not going to stop. An intentional brush alongside the provider or a purposeful flick of the provider's hair will be the move that cannot be denied.

The dad will not stop until the provider clearly says she is not interested. Being married does not matter to a dad with a crush. He will pursue the provider any opportunity he gets – unless the husband is home and standing in the room.

Responding with sarcasm and humor does not stop this behavior. If the provider responds with comments that include his wife or her husband, he does not see it as a warning. He sees it as an engagement. He is happy with ANY attention from the provider to keep his fantasy going.

When the provider says something like, "You have to stop it. I want to keep our relationship professional. We need to have a family meeting to discuss this with your wife," the dad often backs off for the moment, but when he comes back into the daycare for the next drop-off or pick-up, he will ask the provider if she is in a better mood. He does not want to stop doing it. It is that simple.

It is at this point where you must be clear and insist he stop the inappropriate behavior or you will terminate. Some providers respond with verbal admonitions but do not attach a termination warning causing the dad to escalate the attempts to engage. If the provider has an open door policy, the dad will drop in unannounced and sneak into the house to watch the provider. I cannot tell you how many times I have heard of providers being in the middle of their day, only to look up and see a creeper dad watching her. They had no idea of how long he was standing there or how often he has done this before.

Unfortunately, once the provider says she is not interested, the dad becomes angry and acts as if he did not do anything and insists the provider misread the situation. He accuses her of making it up or misunderstanding. Once he is shut down, he pulls the children out of the daycare. He is not interested in the provider as a caregiver to his kids, so switching childcare does not affect him in any way.

I have had daycare dads become infatuated with my staff assistants, a daycare parent make advances towards another parent, a staff assistant fixate on one of my daycare dads and my neighbor become attracted to one of my married daycare moms. In all but one of these instances, I lost a daycare kid once the person who was attracted was confronted and told to stop. I confronted my neighbor and had a two-week war before we finally settled it and he knocked it off. The other instances where both parties were affiliated with my business, I lost a kid. It is very disheartening to lose thousands of dollars a year in income because someone else does not respect boundaries and acts upon their fantasies at your expense. None of the situations had a single thing to do with me or my care of the kids, but I am the one who lost out financially.

Be prepared that regardless of how you handle it, when the seeds of attraction are being planted you will most likely lose money. Start looking for replacement children immediately because as soon as you threaten to terminate, the days the respective child will be in your care are limited.

Daycare Whispers…

Trust your gut. If the dad is making you uncomfortable with his words and actions, he is doing it intentionally.

Start interviewing for the slot because he will escalate his behavior.

Have a male around when you directly confront him. Be prepared for him to deny and accuse you of fabricating or misunderstanding.

When a creeper dad is called out, he will quit the daycare. He's not bringing his kid for the child's best interest. Switching childcare will give him an opportunity to behave badly with another woman.

The "Stay-at-Home-Mom Wannabe"

Returning to work after being on maternity leave is an extremely difficult transition for the new mother. She has become accustomed to devoting her every minute to her newborn and family. The prospect of going back to work is overwhelming.

There are many mothers who really do not want to go back to work. They get into a routine with the baby and relish being able to focus solely on their life at home. Some want to stay home because it is easier to be a stay at home mom than it is to be a working mother with all the responsibilities of the home waiting for them the minute they walk in the door after a hard day at work. Some of these mothers become desperate to come up with SOME way to stay home with the baby.

There are some couples who go to war over whether the baby should go to childcare or the mom should stay home. The reason is always about money. The father wants the mom to work because he wants the income. He does not want to be the sole supporter of the family. In this group of parents, some fight like siblings over the fairness of only one parent having to go out and work while the other gets the easy job of staying home. The father does not like the idea that he has to go do a job every day and the mom gets to live off of his hard work and JUST have to care for the baby and house. The mom tries to convince him the work of caring for the baby and the house IS work, but the dad knows that he can have the housework done, meals prepared, laundry folded and the care of the baby whether or not the mom goes to work. He wants the money from the mom's income AND the entire household taken care of, too.

If the dad wins the first battle of this war, the parents will begin interviewing for childcare. The provider may not be aware that this feud is going on and will consider them to be a typical prospective client. The veteran provider will sense something is wrong by the way the parents act toward each other and the kind of expectations the mother has for the baby's care.

These moms look like the picky parent when they first start the interview. They go into minute details of the baby's schedule and exact method of feeding. They constantly ask for assurance if the provider will do it EXACTLY as they say. They have the common concern of how much adult interaction the baby is going to get, but they are desperate to get confirmation that it will be done with exact precision per the mother's instructions. They shun the idea that another child or baby could come first and their baby would have to wait. They come up with medical reasons why the baby cannot wait and why every whimper must be answered immediately.

The dad intercedes in this back and forth and says they will understand if the baby has to wait a bit or if the schedule cannot be met right to the minute. Right in front of the provider the parents will actually argue with each other about what the baby needs and the contradictions will escalate throughout the interview. By the time the interview is over, the provider is convinced the dad is, but the mom is not, on board. Every interview the parents have with other providers will consist of the same scenario. The provider that takes on these parents is always surprised when she gets a call that she was picked because she did not connect with the mom during the interview.

Before the baby starts childcare the mom sends a lot of communication about the baby. The MyChild letter is extensive. The provider gets pages upon pages of instructions and the mom needs to discuss the instructions before the baby begins care. She wants to make sure the provider will commit to her every detail.

The first day drop-off is pretty normal. The mom cries and is very upset about leaving her baby with a stranger. She leaves the front door doing the ugly cry. All day long the provider fields calls, texts and emails from the mom checking up on the baby. When she comes back to pick up the baby, it is quite obvious she has cried most of the day. She calls after hours to ask questions and is not happy if she hears the baby did well or had an average first day.

When the baby returns to daycare the next day the mom reports that the baby was up all night, was gassy and spit up. She describes a hysterical baby who was impossible to settle. If the provider gets a chance to talk to the dad, he will have a completely different story.

The normal mom stops crying at drop off after the third day. The mom who is unwillingly returning to work does not stop crying even as the week comes to an end. She continues to communicate with the provider at an unprecedented level and is not happy with any of the answers she gets. She will increase her expectations in order to counteract the problems she believes are coming from the baby being in daycare. She will often claim the baby has become ill from being at the daycare. No matter what is going on with the baby in care, the mom will not be happy. She has a reason for this behavior and it has nothing to do with appropriate care of the baby. Her motive is to sabotage the daycare.

I have had this mom a few times in my career. The first time I did not recognize what was going on. I sensed the mom did not want to go back to work, but I did not realize the parents were fighting about it. I just thought the dad was laid back and the mom was a high-strung new mother. What tipped me off that this behavior was WAY different than a newbie mom adjusting to bringing her baby to daycare, was her drama-filled drop-off and excessive crying when she picked up. I had never had a mother cry at pick-up, too. She would cry really hard at drop-off every day and showed no sign of letting up. The first week was understandable, but I was starting to get weary of it when it started back up on week two. My daycare parents were running into this mom on both ends of the day and were giving me some pretty strange looks by the end of the week. What the heck was I doing with this family to have this mom so visibly upset every day?

I also got tired of the constant interference during the day. It seemed as if every answer I gave the mom was unacceptable if it was not a pure declaration that I would do whatever, whenever and however she asked. The simple fact there were other children in the house needing care did not matter to her. She was relentless about every single aspect of the baby's care being done exactly as she instructed.

I was getting exhausted listening to how the baby was suffering at home after being with me during the day. After a weekend home with mom he was perfect, but went right back to being in horrible shape after being in daycare. The baby was perfectly fine at my house so I could not understand how he could be sick and in pain when he was at home. He was a perfectly healthy, very normal baby doing very well in care.

I started talking to the mom about whether it was a mistake to have him in care. I had to firmly tell her NO about her constant requests for conferencing to dissect every miniscule detail of his care and feeding. It was overkill and I needed to get to a normal relationship with her or this was not going to work. I was tired of the insinuation that he was suffering when I knew better. She was extremely angry when I told her I would not accommodate her ever-increasing demands. She knew her baby best and she knew what was best for her baby.

The dad was completely different. He was fine with the care and apologized for mom's behavior. He told me the mom was exaggerating about how the baby was at home and said he was not any different at night than he was before he started.

By the end of the second week, the mom showed no signs of settling down. I decided to have a talk with her before she paid me for the next week. I sat her on my couch and told her that in my opinion she needed to stay home with the baby. She agreed but told me the dad would not let her. This is when I found out what was really going on at home. They had been fighting since before the baby was born about her going back to work. Dad was insistent that he was not going to be the only one working. He was a construction worker and she was a hotel manager. They could live off of his salary if they lived modestly, but he wanted a boat, fancy cars and a nice house. He also did not think it was fair that he had to work a hard manual labor job and she got to just take care of one kid and do housework. He offered to quit his job and stay home, but her salary would not cover their basic bills. They were fighting like siblings over who had to do the hard work and who got the easy work. It was not about the baby.

Once I figured out what was going on I was furious with the game the mom had been playing. All the hysterics at drop-off and pick-up were about her not getting her way. She was trying to submarine my care of the kid so that she could prove to the dad that the baby HAD to be home to get good care. She was not winning the war by economics so she tried to convince him the baby was not safe and well cared for. Even a nurse could not care for his son like she could.

I told her it was time to end our relationship. I had his stuff packed up in advance and handed her the baby's spare clothes and leftover supplies along with a receipt. She was thrilled that I quit and left my house for the first time without crying.

Ten minutes later I got a call from the dad. He was screaming at me for quitting. He told me I had no right deciding the baby should be at home with the mom. I told him that he would never find a provider willing to play monkey in the middle with the two of them. I did not appreciate being an unwilling pawn in either of their games. I had a business to run and I was not going to deal with her constant efforts to undermine my care in an effort to convince him that she was the only one to be trusted to take care of the kid.

After that experience, I was able to pick out the parents who were fighting over the mom going back to work. I pay very close attention to the way they are with each other during the interview. If I sense even an iota of dissidence over the baby being in care, I pass on the prospect of caring for the baby. It is too risky to have a parent who gains by proving the provider to be an incompetent caregiver.

Daycare Whispers…

Pay close attention at the interview to how the couples interact regarding mom going back to work.

If Dad is overly accommodating to the group care concept, but Mom seems to be against each aspect, be aware that she will be unhappy from the first day.

If Mom is disproportionately upset for an extended time after starting care, begin talking to her about whether she can manage working outside the home.

If you can spot this parent at the interview, it is best not to take them as clients. It is risky to work with a mother who has a vested interest in you failing at your job.

If you terminate the family, do not do it with Dad in the house. He is going to be very angry.

Grandparents

Grandparent involvement in their grandchildren's lives can bring a unique dynamic to the daycare relationship. This chapter deals with three different aspects of the grandparent impact in a daycare business: former providers, free caregivers and paying clients.

Grandparents as Former Providers

Back in the pioneer days when I started my home childcare, grandparents were very involved in their grandchildren's life. It was not unusual to get a child when they were two-years old because granny was available to care for the child during infancy. Usually this arrangement was free or nearly free.

By the time the child was two, taking care of him became much harder. Grandma coped with this challenge by letting him watch a lot of television and eat a pure junk diet. This resulted in Snowflake becoming even more difficult to watch. Grandma realized it would actually be easier to get a job outside of the house. After all, if she was going to work that hard, she might as well get paid. Most of these parent/grandparent breakups were amicable. The parents wanted a little more structure, but they were feeling the results of grandma's leniency in their own home. They had a good deal for a good long while and they respected that it could not go on forever.

The age of the child leaving free granny care started to decline in the late nineties. I started to see more 18-month olds needing care. In the early 2000s, I saw more 12-month olds and by the mid-2000s, depending on when the baby started crawling, I was interviewing many more parents of 7-9 month olds in this situation.

I have a theory of one of the reasons why grandmas started giving up taking care of the grandkids earlier in the baby's life... the World Wide Web. The grandmas started to get the internet around the early to mid-2000s. They had more to entertain themselves at home and caring for a grandkid for free was harder to do while they were on the computer. Television was the biggest distraction before WWW, but watching a baby and soap operas at the same time was not too laborious. Playing on the internet and watching a baby was much more challenging. The internet offered another life and Grandma liked it.

As soon as the baby became mobile, granny surrendered. I had many years when I got a new baby for both day and night shift around the sixth to eighth month. By the late 2000s, the number of inquiries I received for infants who had been with grandma was very few and far between. My daycare friends saw the same trends. Kids who had been with grandma during their infancy became more of anomaly.

The transition from unpaid granny care to group care used to be the hardest daycare transition of all. Babies and toddlers who were cared for by grandma took way longer to go native because they were used to having the highest level of one-to-one care available. They are often indulged and spoiled. Who wants you to be happier more than ANYONE on the planet? Your grandmother.

I was at full capacity in some points of my daycare life to where I was able to turn away any baby who had been with grandma. I did not want the cryfest for the first three months of care when the baby was removed from the center of the universe to one of the orbiting moons. Now with current parenting methods of attachment and permissive parenting, there is not much difference between a baby who has been home exclusively with mom and one that used to be home with grandma.

Some grandmas are registered or licensed through the state and receive compensation for caring for their grandchildren via childcare grants. Daycare provider grandmas are more likely to care for their grandchildren as daycare kids. It is becoming unusual to find grandchildren being cared for by grandmothers who are not already operating a childcare or not receiving state funding as compensation. Children leaving paid granny care going into a regular daycare setting can be a blessing to childcare providers as they tend to behave better and the transition to the group setting is easier.

The Free GrannyCare Cycle

There is a subset of the parent population still using grandma to care for the babies. These are often parents who make too much to qualify for assistance, but too little to pay for decent daycare. These parents need help and if grandma is willing to do it for free (or near free), it is a great deal.

With this generation of entitlement and grandma having a life outside of her family, the relationships can become rocky. If a parent takes advantage of grandma by using the free care for extra hours, bringing the kids in their jammies and night diaper, forgetting basic supplies like diapers, wipes and food, and expecting the grandma to do her normal grandma duties of additional weekend and evening, the grandma will burn out quickly. (Just think of your worst behaving client and then envision caring for their children for free!) Once the grandma starts putting her foot down and refusing to be walked on, the parents get upset. If the grandma starts expecting money, then the parents start placing demands on what she is to do with the children when they are with her. They want trips to the park, education and little to no TV. The next step is when they start telling sob stories of how they are broke and cannot make their daycare payment. Grandma knows better because she is in the front row seat watching how they spend their money. Once the debt becomes high enough, she either starts expecting the parents to do work around the house for free to barter away the bill.

The parent wants the daycare situation back the way it used to be and refuses to give ANYTHING to the grandma. They do not live up to their promises of in-kind work and they do not want to give up their money. Most of all, they refuse to respect her role as grandma and mom and will not show even a little bit of gratitude for what she is doing for them.

The grandma often retaliates by requiring the parents to pay full price for daycare. She does a bit of snooping around and finds out the going rate. She figures out what she is giving away for free and she expects the parents to finally start paying it. When THIS day comes, the whole thing blows to smithereens. The parents figure if they are going to have to pay for daycare they would rather pay a non-relative because, unlike with Grandma, they can hire a stranger who will do what they are told. They pull the kids out of grandma's care and hire a daycare provider who will start immediately. In retaliation they often tell Grandma she cannot see the kids at all, not even on evenings and weekends.

When a parent who has had free or near-free grandma care comes to the daycare interview, they have a lot to say about how it did not work out with Grandma. They complain about how much television the kids watched, the terrible diets, the long naps and how the kids behaved in the evening. They want to rectify all of this in their new childcare relationship.

What they do not share with the provider is that the cost of grandma was free. The provider does not realize that the parents have had a long history of being able to use all of their money for regular life bills and expenses and most likely have extra money for entertainment and eating out. The provider does not see how this history will dramatically affect her by the end of the first month.

The parents now have to pay a significant portion of their salary to childcare. They are able to come up with the first few weeks out of their paychecks, but it does not take long before they feel the full financial impact of this new arrangement. When they do not have enough money to pay the bills, much less anything extra, grandma care starts to look a whole lot better than it did a few weeks ago. It is at this point where the provider begins to have serious issues with the parents coming up short or delaying payments. They pay their other bills first and start complaining about any little thing that goes wrong with the kid or invent problems if they cannot find any.

They begin to call the grandma again and bit by bit start telling her about how their Pookie and Snowflake miss her SO much. They tell her the children ask every day if they are going to go to Grandma's and cry nonstop when told no. They have the children call Grandma to tell her how much they miss her. Eventually, they tell Grandma that the new provider is not taking good care of the kids and may even be mean to them. This is when apologizing and admitting they were wrong begins. They tell Grandma how no one will ever take care of the Pookster and Snow like she does. They are afraid to take the kids to daycare because they have a feeling the kids are being neglected. They say they would rather pay Grandma than this provider and ask if she will take the kids back. Grandma feels vindicated and believes her grandkids are at risk. She finally gets her first real "thank you" out of the parents. All she wanted was a little money and some consideration. She finally feels the parents respect her and appreciate what she has done for them.

Meanwhile, the provider has no idea all of this is going on in the background. All she knows is the parents are late on the fees. When the kids just do not show up on payday she starts to figure something is wrong because she knows the parents have to go to work. Unfortunately, the provider got caught up in the free granny cycle. When she demands payment for past due fees and payment for notice time to which the parents agreed, she is punished with a complaint to the state. The parents believe if she is investigated by the state that they will get out of paying what they owe.

The free granny care experience is awful for the provider. She spent time interviewing the family believing they were seeking the best care for their child because they are giving up Grandma... (You know it had to be bad if they were firing Grandma!) She has given one or two slots of her business and turned away other prospects. She has done the HARD work of trying to integrate one or two kids who have been with Grandma. She does not get paid for the work she has already done, nor does she receive notice time pay. She also gets investigated by the state on the trumped up allegations. A trip to small claims court is the only way to get the monies owed.

It was one month of daycare hell that she never saw coming. The only solace is she will most likely win her court case. It will only take three weeks before grandma is right back to where she started with the parents. Once they get her sucked back into their gig they will shed their promises and gratitude. The cycle will begin again and last until she has had enough. Then the parents will go again to another unsuspecting provider to bridge the gap in the free grandma care cycle.

When you get a call from a family needing care for children who have been with grandma, ask the hard questions. The first question is how much they paid her. Next find out how long she has provided their care and listen closely to their complaints. If their concerns have been going on nearly the whole time the kids have been with her, then ask why they did not leave her a long time ago. If they are squirmy when answering, you will know they did it only to save the money.

Look at the fee you are going to charge them and think about how much impact this big bill will have on their lives. It's not the same as having a large car payment or mortgage. If they have been able to get by without having to pay this kind of money, how long do you think it is going to be before they want their old deal back? They can tell you the relationship with Grandma is over, but when they have to choose between making some consolations with Grandma and paying out all that money, they are going to choose sucking it up with Grandma.

They may tell you the reason why Grandma surrendered is because she got a job. Grandmas often tell their mooching children they are going to get a job. This is to get them out the door without too big of a fight. If Grandma is in her fifties or early sixties, she knows it's not going to be so easy for her to just go out and score a job, but she will say or do whatever it takes to change the situation.

If you do have openings and want to take the risk of taking in kids formerly in grandma care, require the contract be notarized, a minimum two-week deposit, a full month of notice time and all weekly payments in advance. If they are late on one payment, do not allow them back without catching up. If they offer partial payment the third payday (this is a common time for them to start running low on money), take a partial payment, but do not offer another day of service not paid for in advance. Do not let them pay behind.

Keep interviewing prospective clients. There's a good chance you will have empty slots very soon. Keep documentation of any issues that come up with the children and make them sign and date any communication regarding any issues. You will need them when the state inspector investigates their complaint.

If you can afford to pass on them, you may want to consider it. You have to ask yourself if the inevitable complaint inspection is worth the money you will receive while they are sorting out and resetting their deal with grandma.

Grandparents as Clients

I have worked for a few grandparents and it has been a very good experience. If the grandparents have custody of their grandkids and receive state funding, it works out really well. If they have to pay out of pocket, it is a bit harder. They can feel resentful of the fees when it is not for their own children.

If the parents are still involved in the child's life it can get messy. It's hard to know who your client is if the mom or dad start placing expectations on the provider. They can also have ups and downs with the parents wherein at times the parent is welcome to come see the kids and at others they forbid it. The provider can often be in the middle of that tug-o-war.

Sometimes the grandparents will pull the children out of care if they have previously allowed visits, but have decided they no longer want the parents to see the kids. They may go as far as to switch daycares in order to have the kids in a home the parents do not know and cannot visit. If you can avoid onsite parent visits, it may save you from being termed.

The advantage of working with grandparents is that they are usually older and more settled. They are more mature and understand your job is hard. If they have full custody they are not as lenient as they would be if they were just allowed to be the doting grandparents. They pay on time and are respectful of the arrival and departure times. However, there may be times they are overwhelmed with the responsibility of caring for another generation of children and the fatigue can work its way into the relationship with the provider. If they have many appointments for the children with lawyers and social workers, you may have to deal with unusual schedules. If social workers want to visit the children, they may ask if they can do so at childcare.

My experience is that younger grandparents fare a bit better than the older grandparents. They are still deep into their own career and have not had much of a break from work. Older grandparents are used to time off and having such a huge difference in age between them and the young grandchildren can lead to permissiveness and allowances of activities like television, gaming and tablets. They have a hard time keeping up with them, so they leave them in care for the maximum allowable hours.

Daycare Whispers...

Be on alert for the "free granny cycle" parents.

Take extra precautions to solidify their contract by having it notarized and setting a lengthy notice of termination.

Be aware that the end of the first month, when a parent's main bills are due, will be the time the relationship goes south.

Keep vigilant documentation of any parental concerns and have the parents sign it when it is resolved.

With grandparents as clients, know they may have resentment for having to care and pay for the grandkids. They may accept your rates until they find someone cheaper.

Be prepared to do open to close hours for the grandchildren - especially if the grandparent is significantly older than the child.

The Terminated Parent

Even the most seasoned veteran childcare provider hates to terminate a family. It is very stressful and the worst part of terminating comes after the parents are given the notice. The days before the termination are a time of financial worry and soul searching. The uncertainty of whether a new, better behaving family can be acquired is daunting.

Better the devil you know than the devil you don't? Finding clients who are excellent parents and are caring and kind with the provider is becoming increasingly difficult. Golden parents are nearing extinction and the average provider only lasts two years in this business. If she does not find the special sauce to attract the cream of the crop parents, she often surrenders shortly after starting.

I have twenty years in this business. This is ten times the number of years the average provider survives. In two decades of caring for kids, I have had to terminate around five or six families. I had a few ugly terminations, but I learned over time how to do it and when to surrender to the inevitable fact that no matter what I did, it was going to be a bad experience.

I had two full-house terminations when I sold my home to move. They went better than the other terminations, but it was still very difficult. I had one family who was terribly upset and it made the final days of caring for the child a roller coaster of hard feelings. I had given them a full month's notice with the final week being a week I was already planning a vacation. They felt it was not long enough and that I had misled them by not disclosing my house was on the market. In contrast, the other families were very happy for me and wished me well on my new adventure. This experience taught me that no matter how you make changes, you are always going to have someone who feels you did it wrong.

When a termination is a singular event, the dynamics are very different than closing down the business. When you close down your business, the individual parents do not feel targeted. They may not be happy, but most do not take it personally. The ones who become angry will fixate on the way you did it as opposed to what you did. They will insist you should have told them earlier what your plans were, you should have given more time, you should have told them before they enrolled that you were considering moving, etc. Most "should haves" are about them feeling duped.

If a provider tells parents well in advance she is thinking about shutting down she will have a mass exodus of clients long before she can afford to close the daycare. It is never in a provider's best interest to give more notice than she expects to get when a contract is ending. If you require a two-week notice, then give a two-week notice. If you require a month, give a month. It is easier for a family to find a childcare provider than for a childcare provider to find a family. There are some geographical exceptions, but in the US and Canada there are millions of empty childcare slots to be had.

The vast majority of the time the parents will find a new childcare long before they have to - especially if given a month's notice. The last move I made, my clients found care within two days. Be prepared for the notice you have given to be unneeded. Know that many parents are going to want to get out of paying for the time they do not use in the notice. They tell the provider that the new provider insisted they start right away or the slot will not be available. I recommend allowing them to pull out when they find care. It is not worth it to enforce notice time for a termination you initiated. It ends the relationship on an unnecessary bad note.

How quickly a family finds care is directly proportional to the deal they are getting with the current provider. If the provider is cheap, allows variable schedules, only charges for the days the child attends and requires pay after services are rendered instead of prepaying, it is going to take time to replicate that great deal. If the parents are paying a hefty fee for care, have fixed schedules and pay upfront for care, they can find a new daycare very quickly. My clients find care within days because there are legions of providers willing to take high paying kids with golden parents.

If the provider is taking a beating on every aspect of time and money, the parents will stay until the last minute she offers care. It takes time to find someone willing to do so much for so little. The very last day the family is in care they will often be REALLY late picking up. I have heard stories of parents who were supposed to pick-up at 4 p.m. not showing up until 9:30 at night. They do not answer their phones and when they finally do, they tell the provider they were out looking for childcare. They want to have the final word and they know the provider cannot do a thing about it.

Compared to shutting down a daycare, terminating a family is a different beast. This family knows the daycare is still up and running, but they are no longer welcome. This means you are firing them. They have a hard time accepting the matrix of your position because they often believe they are the boss and you are the employee. How can an employee fire the boss? The undercurrent that you need the money has given this parent many concessions and tolerance for bad behavior. Once the termination letter hits their inbox they realize you do not need or want their money. Now how can they continue to behave badly if you do not want their money?

Parents want to break up with you. They do not want you breaking up with them. It is this desire to be the one in charge that leads to a common set of behaviors with a very predictable pattern. It is good to know the cycle so you can use it to your advantage.

Most infant terminations are due either to an infant requiring one-on-one care in order to not cry all day long or parents not abiding by the policies of the business. Most toddler and preschooler terminations are because the child is becoming violent or the parent is not complying with the policies. Most school-aged terminations are because the child is violent, destructive and requires a level of supervision that surpasses all the children in care combined.

Parents are offended when their infant is terminated because they are unable to adapt to the childcare environment. They are surprised despite being well apprised the baby was crying all day long and would only stop when having their own adult. They immediately feel the provider is incompetent: if she cannot keep the baby from crying, then the baby is unsafe in her care.

At first the parent will attempt to bargain with the provider to reconsider. To the provider they are apologetic and swear they will start dealing with the demanding baby. But behind closed doors they are furious and will immediately start searching for another provider. They only promise to deal with the demanding baby because they need daycare the next day. They have absolutely no intention of fixing the problem.

Some providers are relieved that the parent is finally listening to them about their concerns and offer to restart the relationship with a mutual pact to work together. This is a crucial mistake. Once you tell an infant's mother you cannot deal with the crying, she does not want her child with you. She will use you until she finds someone else, but as soon as she does, she will claim that she is worried about safety as you may snap on the baby. This worry only surfaces after they find a new daycare unless they already have someone who could care for the baby while they look. If they have Grandma waiting in the wings, they will immediately pull the baby out of the daycare.

The termination of the toddler and preschooler is almost always because of violent behavior or crying. Occasionally a provider will term for a medical condition she is unable to manage. I have also seen a trend of termination of new one-year olds if they are able to get out of the current sleeping equipment. Over the last few years, the manufacturers of infant equipment have downsized the pack-n-plays and cribs. The pack-n-plays available at the beginning of my career were six-inches deeper than the ones made today. Six inches is a full two years of growth in the average child.

The old equipment easily housed kids until they turned three. Now the new one-year olds can lift their legs over the side. If the provider cannot contain the new one-year old during nap, she will sometimes terminate. She cannot directly supervise the child for two naps a day. Giving up nap breaks along with dealing with crying are very common precursors to terminations.

School-aged children are termed because they can rock a provider's world. They are big enough, strong enough and mouthy enough to take over a home provider. They can easily harm the children and the provider and they can make up fantastical stories to get their way. The amount of care a badly behaved school-ager takes can be more than all the other children in the daycare combined.

Termination for parental behavior is much more common than terminating because of the child's behavior. It is common to have issues with both parents and kids at the same time, but it is just as common to have no issues with the child while having severe issues with the parents. It is extremely rare to terminate a family with an awesome set of parents and a child who is unworkable.

In my career, I have had one medical termination and the rest were parental behavior terminations. I have not had a child I could not manage. I have also developed policies in the business to essentially force out families. When I did not want to terminate, I just developed policies they would not abide by and they left willingly.

The cycle of termination begins with parental bargaining and abiding by the rules while they are seeking other childcare. If the parent has talked the provider into trying to try work out the relationship, the provider will not realize the parent is on the hunt. Her first indication is usually when the old issues start creeping back into the picture. If you have termed a parent and agreed to try over and the issues you termed them for come back up, you can be 100% certain they have found other daycare. They may not tell you because they do not want to risk any money they have prepaid.

The day the prepaid money is used up is the day the provider gets the termination from the parent. They feel vindicated because even though they were recently terminated, they get to be the one to term after they reset the relationship with promises to be compliant. This is the natural order they were seeking in the first place. They are the boss and they do the firing.

When parents blindside the provider with the termination, she first and foremost wants the contracted notice money. This is where the termination war erupts. The parent does not feel the provider deserves any notice. The accusations begin that the provider is incompetent and they are in fear of their child's life. They often say they changed their mind because they do not believe the provider likes their child. The truth is they just found a new daycare but admitting that would not get them out of the termination notice time. If they claim the child is in danger, then they believe it is ok to leave.

This termination scenario always ends in a big blow out over the provider returning all supplies and a text message war of every complaint the provider and parent had during the relationship. It ends with a phone call to the State where the parents turn the provider in. They know the best and biggest revenge they can have on the provider is an unannounced visit from the State and a permanent complaint on the provider's record.

The parent who is termed and unable to weasel their way into starting over with the provider gets very angry when the bargaining does not work. They go from shocked to bargaining and then to anger. The provider starts getting messages like "your behavior is and has been disappointingly unprofessional." They will continue to use the daycare if they do not have any other way to go to work. The drop-offs and pick-ups are brutal in that the provider gets the silent treatment and some door slamming. The parent communicates with the provider by talking to the child in front of the provider instead of directly to the provider.

The situation escalates very quickly. It is not unusual to have it erupt just a few days into the notice time. If the provider is disrespected in front of her children and daycare children she wants to end the relationship right away. The parents who know they are on the outs start breaking every policy the provider has that they know will make her mad. They come late at pick-up and allow their child to bring in toys and drinks, despite knowing it is not allowed. They believe the provider has to allow the full notice and they have nothing to lose by breaking the rules.

The provider decides the money she is receiving for the last week is not worth dealing with the bad behavior so she ends the relationship early. The parent does not see this coming and becomes furious. The provider tells them point blank they cannot come back and the parent goes ballistic.

Depending on where the parent and provider are when the final blow occurs, the situation can become scary. If the provider does the termination in her home, the parent will not hold back their anger. They will cuss, accuse, threaten and get up in the provider's face. They do not care if children are present or not.

If the provider does the termination over the phone, the parents will blow up her phone with texts and messages. They will call repeatedly with their demands. They want every stitch of every single thing they have left at the daycare. If the provider does not give back everything they think is at the daycare it can lead to more calls and texts. I have heard stories of parents coming back to the provider's home demanding a missing sock or pacifier. They will use any excuse to get the provider face to face.

Sometimes it is better to give immediate terminations and not bother with notice time. If the termination is over poor parental behavior, the behavior you terminate for will be nothing compared to the behavior which surfaces once they are termed. It is a hard thing to be able to foresee how they are going to react, but it is worth considering just ending the relationship. If you do not want them back, then pack their kids belongings, have another adult present and step out the door with them to give them the news. Make sure you have everything in the go home bags so they do not have a reason to come back. Have their receipt and a refund of any unused daycare fees in the bag.

Not every termination ends this way. Sometimes the parents are upset but they keep it together until the last day. I have heard of providers terminating and the parents talking the provider into allowing the kid to stay with promised changes and it has worked out. In my experience, this is rare, but it can happen.

I have developed a terminating routine over the decades of doing childcare that is a bit different. I do not have clients that would act aggressive with me or act up in front of children. When I give a termination, I tell the parent that the arrangement is not working and offer them free childcare until they find other care. I do not put a time limit on how long they have to search. If it takes a month then they get a free month of daycare. If it takes three months then they get three months of free daycare.

I do this because I want to send them the message that from that minute forward I will not take another penny from them. We no longer have a financial relationship. I am offering free care to afford them time to look for care and put together any deposits they need for the next arrangement. I do not work for them or with them. They must behave as perfect angels to get this free offering. If they even tweak my sensibilities, they leave that day.

I have offered this twice and both families left that day. They could not manage our relationship if, in their minds, they were not the boss. They knew they would not be able to work with me under my terms and behave. You would think that someone who was perfectly happy with my services the day before would gladly take free care the day after the termination, but they did not. I know they will not when I offer it. They think by leaving right away they are punishing me by withholding their kid from me. They think their child is unsafe in my care if I do not take their money. Mostly, they want the final word even if it means giving up a great deal in order to give it. I am cool with that. It is built into the offer.

I can afford to offer that in a termination. I do it so that the situation does not escalate and the parents feel like they are in charge when they refuse it. The departure is tense, but not ugly. They do, however, turn me into the State. I always make a phone call to my licensing worker before I terminate. When the investigator comes for the complaint inspection I answer the door with "I was expecting you. Come on in." I always send a copy of the complaint inspection to the family. I tell them when they leave that I will do this. That way they know I know they are going to call the State.

There is a wide breadth of advice given on what to put in writing in terminations. I do not write termination letters. I tell them either on the phone or in person. If you choose to write a termination letter then consider that however you do it, they are going to be angry. If you write a letter that simply says, "services are no longer available after such and such date" with no explanation of why, the parents are going to be angry that you did not give them a reason. If you outline why you are terminating then they are going to be angry about what your reasons are. It does not matter how you word it. You are breaking up with them. They want to be the ones breaking up with you. You cannot win either way.

I suggest writing a termination letter like the one I have at the beginning of the book. It makes you feel SO good to put everything down and read it over and over. It is fun to read to your provider friends. Once you have it out of your system then write the real termination letter. It does not do anyone any good to hammer a family when they are leaving. It is best to keep it short and sweet.

The only exception to this is medical terminations. If a child has a medical condition you are unable to serve, it is best to include that in the letter. It covers you if the child becomes injured or dies as a result of the issue you were concerned about. It is proof that you brought the condition to the parents and that you were unable to properly care for the child. If you are challenged by human services or are asked to be a witness in a trial, you have the proof that you addressed the medical condition with the parents.

One other technique I have used to avoid termination is to not offer a contract to a family until they have been with me for three to six months. I allow families to leave without notice or obligation during this time with the understanding I can do the same. If I feel the parents are not working out then I force the contract at a time when I know they will not sign it. This is usually right before I take a vacation. If the situation is rocky, they will not be happy contracting to pay my vacation time and the contract pushes them over the edge. They decline to go on contract and they end the relationship themselves.

This technique is risky if you need a set income and notice. I am able to use this technique because I do not. I can easily replace families and I do not want to get locked into a family and have to go through the drama to terminate them early in our relationship. I have had two forced contract terminations that resulted in them leaving without calling the State after they left. This is a good way to end a bad relationship.

Daycare Whispers...

It does not matter what reasoning you give for termination. The parent will be upset if you give specific reasons or no reasons at all.

If you give a reason, they will be angry at the reason. If you give no reason, they will be angry that you did not give them a reason.

Do not expect parents to stay through your own notice time after a termination.

Secure your income for as many days as possible before giving the termination letter.

Always, always, always, always be prepared for a full State inspection after a termination.

If you believe the parent will get nasty and possibly violent, do the termination when they are not in the home.

Have a backup adult available when you are doing terminations.

Give the same notice you expect to get when you are closing down.

Bonus Footage: Daycare Whisperer Techniques

Open Door Policy

The old saying of a good offense is the best defense is true when dealing with any of the parental behaviors mentioned in this book. One of the best ways to ensure you have good parents (or better behaving parents) is to understand and manage the open door expectations of the parents and the state in which you reside.

The open door policy is often misunderstood. Most people believe it is a "mi casa es su casa" policy.

This is not true.

Each state requires childcare providers to have an open door policy. This is often interpreted that any time the child is in the home, the parents must have access to their child, the home and anything and everyone on the property. Providers should read their state code to understand whether it gives the parents the right to stay on the property and have access to everything associated or if the parent simply has to have immediate access to their child at any time.

Parents are not allowed to free-range my home. All arrivals and departures occur at the front door, which is always locked. The parents stay at the front entryway when they arrive with their child and again when they pick up in the afternoon. The children must also remain at the front entryway at arrival and departure as long as the parents are in my home.

My front door is in the living room and other than basic safety proofing, such as covered outlets, is not a child-proofed area. This is an intentional design. I do not want any playing going on when parents are dropping off and picking up and I especially do not want parents sitting down on my couch and visiting while their child plays. At arrival, I want to get to my work. At departure, I want to get the kid out the door as quickly as possible.

Get in.
Get out.
Get paid.

I have had legions of parents who would not consider my childcare because I will not allow unbridled access to my entire home at any time they desire.

Many parents look for childcare where they can visit the playroom at any time and stay as long as they want any time the childcare is open. They also want to be able to have access to the provider's entire house. They believe if their child is in the home they have the right to check out everything under the roof. Those parents will not hire me and I am good with that.

The first thing parents learn about managing their child in daycare from books, magazines, and childcare referrals is to always drop in unannounced, stay and observe. Parents are encouraged to come at times when the provider does not expect them and are given the impression that the willingness of the provider to allow this is a make-or-break deal. If the provider does not allow these unannounced visits, they should find another provider.

During the interview process, the parents see the childcare areas three times before their child begins care. They see each area where their child will be during different times of the day. I do interviews late in the afternoon when I have one or two children in the daycare. I want them to meet my staff assistant as well as see a few of the kids and their parents when they tour. Not only does this give them the ability to meet parents with whom they could visit with regarding my reference, it also provides ample opportunity for them to see the operational set up of the daycare. If, at any time, they should want to see it again, I would make arrangements for them to come when I did not have other kids in the house. They are welcome to see the childcare rooms weekly if that makes them feel more comfortable. I do not allow them to revisit the rooms when the other children are onsite unless it is to count heads. I will allow them to verify the number of children in the house at any given time. However, if they linger to assess more than the number of kids, I will intercede and ask them to leave.

Parents should be able to come at any time to get their child. I allow one arrival and one departure per family per day. The only exception is if the child has a mid-day, specialty doctor appointment. Otherwise, parents who come at an unscheduled time are required to take their child with them. If they have multiple children, they must take them all. I do not allow a visit before they take their child. They must leave quickly so I can return to work.

I have a security camera at the driveway and when I see a parent's car arrive I fetch their child and take them to the front door. Consequently, the parent sees the child within seconds of arriving and my obligation to give them immediate access is fulfilled. I dress the child quickly and they scoot on out the door. I do not do parent conferencing at pick-up time. If the parents want to visit about something, I will call them when I am not busy. I love it when kids are picked up early. I encourage parents to drop by unannounced for an early pick up. I want them to come when I least expect it so they can instantly see their child is always well cared for.

Parents in the Playroom

I do not interpret the open door policy to mean that parents can visit the OTHER children in the childcare. I am not in the business of hosting free play dates for the parents to enjoy. I do not get paid enough to host play dates. If they want to see their child interacting with other children they can host their own get-togethers with their friends and family. They can go to fast food restaurants, the park and kiddie fun centers. My business is not the place to have this life experience with their child.

Every provider has to decide what level of access parents will have to their home and the other kids. I do not want parents parenting their children under my roof. I do not want the parents to become attached to the other children. I do not want them to pick up the babies or discipline the other kids. I do not want them watching my helper work or listening in on our conversations. I do not want them watching my parenting of my child in our home. I do not want them witnessing diaper changes or discipline of other children. I do not want them to distract children from play or eating.

My main reason for not including the parents in the play and care of the other children is that it can never make me money. I do childcare to make money.

Nothing good can come of a relationship between the parents and the children of my other clients inside the daycare. It can, however, become a liability. Once parents start engaging in the play of the other children, they begin to make judgments about the other kids, the environment and the way the provider runs the business. They ask personal questions about the other families and my refusal to answer causes conflict and unease. They want to know what days the others attend, do they play with their kid, what their parents do for a living, etc.

Over time, the parents in my childcare run into each other at arrival or departure and they see each other's kids. This works out beautifully as long as they keep the meeting outside of my home. I do not mind a little visiting when they first see each other, but I do not want to host a get-to-know-you visit inside my home. I want them all to go to work or go home. As parents meet, they often extend their relationship to social media.

While they are interested in the age-mates of their child, parents are especially interested in the older kids. They like the idea of their kid playing with older children. They know in their personal life that their child is very happy when playing with older kids - especially if there is a two year or more difference in age. Most parents believe their child plays well with the older kids because their child is gifted or advanced. This is an incorrect notion. Even developmentally delayed kids prefer an older child. The older child is more entertaining. Every kid, every day, wants to play with the most exciting kid – which is found in the ones who are older.

As much as a parent wants their child to play with one who is two years older, they are not interested in their child playing with kids two years younger. They never stop to think that the parents of the older kids are not pleased with the notion that their child is stuck playing with a kid two years younger.

The attachment to the older kids can cause problems in your business. The older kids age out first. When the day comes that the older kid goes off to preschool or kindergarten, the parent is upset because their kid is losing their best friend and entertainer. They often consider removing their kid from your care to either follow the older kid to a preschool or to go into a center where there are preschool kids their own age or older. If you do not manage the parent's attachment, you will lose kids prematurely.

One of the ways to manage a parent's affection for the other children in the daycare is to keep the parents out of the playroom and away from the relationship between the kids. ALWAYS promote the relationship between their child and the YOUNGER kids. When you discuss the other kids, always talk about how their kid is buddies with the younger kids. The younger kids may leave, but the likelihood of this is considerably less than that of the older children. If the younger kid leaves, the parents barely give it a second glance because they do not consider it a loss to their child.

It is in the best interest of the business not to discuss kids leaving unless it is obvious they are going to school or their child knows the child will no longer be attending daycare. If the parents do not bring it up, neither should the provider. I have had kids be gone for three months before the parents realize the child is no longer attending. This is ideal because the parent sees that the kid leaving did not affect their child. If the parent is allowed in the playroom, they will know all the details of the comings and goings. That will never make you money.

Another reason I do not allow parents in the playroom is because the kids act like little fools when they have an audience. Kids can sense the change in energy as the provider becomes nervous and worries about disciplining and children crying. The provider's behavior naturally escalates when her paycheck is on the line. The children use any opportunity they can get to escalate themselves because they know it will go unchecked or the provider will minimize her response. They will put the provider to the test if they sense an iota of weakness. A provider is weak when the parents are around because each parent represents a significant percentage of her salary. This threat of loss can affect her ability to support her own children.

The only advantage to allowing parents in the playroom is to get them in the door of your business. I am willing to lose all the prospective clients that require me to allow random access. I explain to them that the other children's parents do not want strange adults around their child. I also encourage them to consider that I cannot run a full child abuse or criminal check on each parent weekly. I do not know for certain that other parents are perfectly safe around their kid. It takes time to get to know a family and I do not want to take any chances with giving direct access to their child just because another parent can afford a slot in my daycare.

Home childcare providers are often alone caring for kids. The normal course of caring for kids can leave opportunities for the visiting parent to gain access to a child, even if it is for a brief moment. Just because someone has the title of parent and has the ability to enroll their child in childcare, does not make them safe. Our prisons and mental health institutions are chock full of parents. I do not have the skill set to ensure an incoming parent is safe to be around the other kids. I prefer to remain cautious and keep the parents away from each other's kids unless they are with their parents during drop-off or pick-up.

If you do allow parents in the playroom I urge you to make sure the parent does not have anything on them that could harm a child. I have heard countless stories of parents dropping coins, lighters, pen lids, pills and rocks from their shoes onto the playroom floor. If a small child ingests something from the floor, you are responsible regardless of who brought it into the room.

If a parent falls over on a child or drops a child you have allowed them to hold, you are responsible. If the parent falls on your property, you are always liable. This is a huge consideration when deciding how far into the home to allow parents. One year I calculated how many additional trips up and down my stairway I would have if I had parents delivering their kids to and from the playrooms. With the capacity I have had in the twenty years of doing childcare, I calculated the parent trips on the stairwells in my two locations would have totaled over 300,000 for just arrival and departure. When you think about it over the course of a career, you have to keep in mind that with having parents scale your stairs that many times, the odds are high that you are going to have an accident as well as significant wear and tear on that area. If a parent falls while holding their child, it could devastate your business. Even with insurance, one claim can make it impossible to get insurance in the future. In addition, your mortgage company may call in your mortgage if you are not properly insured. When you add in the likely factor of the parent parenting their child on the way up and down the stairs you markedly increase the chances of them or their child having a fall. After seeing thousands of incidences of kids behaving badly with their parents on the twenty-foot walk between their car and my front door, I am certain the chances of a stairway fall would be quite high. It only takes one to put you out of business.

Daycare Whispers...

Check with your state regarding whether the open door policy means you must leave doors unlocked.

You do not have to host parents parenting their child onsite.

Allow parents to do a head count at any time.

Parents can come unannounced to fetch their child, but they do not have to have access to the other kids.

If the parent comes at an odd time, answer the door with the child in your arms and scoot them out the door.

One arrival, one departure, per family, per day.

Consult with the Daycare Whisperer

Tori Fees R.N., B.S.N. is the Daycare Whisperer. As an experienced childcare provider, private nanny, registered nurse, expert witness and daycare consultant, Tori offers childcare related consultation for parents, providers, center owners, law enforcement, and attorneys.

Home Childcare Provider Consultation

Daycare providers everywhere have many demands in their day. The Daycare Whisperer understands the intrinsic challenges all home daycare providers experience. The Daycare Whisperer offers one-on-one private consultation with daycare providers via the telephone with respect to any problem you might be facing with regard to parental conflict and child health and behavior management. Many daycare providers assume that networking via internet forums or with colleagues will offer them solutions to their problems. However, this assumption is a misnomer. Often times those who answer forum requests for help are not experts with experience in the field of home daycare. It is impossible to know how successful the adviser actually is in her business or if she has even done childcare for more than a few months or years.

The Daycare Whisperer assists home daycare providers with many facets of their businesses. Providers who have used the services of the Daycare Whisperer have found they have less conflict with parents and experience better behaved, more easily managed children in their care.

The Daycare Whisperer offers the additional following services to home daycare providers:

- Parental conflict resolution
- Rates and fees
- Contract review and rewrite

- Policy review and rewrite
- Scheduling for infants and toddlers
- Nap/rest time solutions
- Infant transitions
- Feeding issues for any age
- Behavior management and problems
- ADA compliancy and rights of the provider
- How the ADA affects your daycare
- Daycare set up and toy requirements
- Transitioning to healthy, organic eating
- Hiring and managing staff assistants
- Dealing with Daycare and Protective Services complaints
- Termination letters

Daycare Center Consultation

Tori, the Daycare Whisperer, has proven to be an integral part of daycare center operations and staff involvement. Tori maintains a current and thorough understanding of Daycare and Protective Services standards and protocol, parental expectations and legalities surrounding daycare center operations.

The Daycare Whisperer specializes in consultation and assistance to daycare centers. Daycare Whisperer's services regarding daycare center video monitoring has been shown to dramatically increase staff productivity, reduce operational costs and increase safety standards.

Daycare Center Testimonial:

Our daycare center has been using the Daycare Whisperer's services since March, 2010. We own and operate two large daycare centers in central Iowa serving children from birth to age twelve. Our center carries an enrollment of 463 children at full capacity and employs 80 staff members. We offer video and audio surveillance in every child-occupied room.

While operating a large daycare center, every owner realizes the liability that comes with such a tremendous responsibility. Tori has been instrumental in assisting our center with lower liability costs. The video monitoring service is crucial to our monitoring of staff interactions with the children. In areas of special concern, such as rooms with multiple parental complaints, Tori focuses on that room and pinpoints the specific deficiencies of staff members which helps our center to immediately correct the problem. Our center is able to use the feedback from Tori regarding the video footage and time-stamped reporting to train staff on specific problems areas needing attention. Video monitoring has also served to be tremendously beneficial with concern to disciplinary action of staff members. This video reporting supports any employer claims with respect to employee infractions, thereby lessening employment claims.

Tori has also allowed us to identify and praise talented staff and star employees when considering staff promotions and wage increases. The staff has responded favorably to Tori's input as they understand she is there to help and promote excellent care and hard work. Tori's willingness to speak to staff in real time as issues arise is a direct benefit to the care of the children and the structure and operation of the classroom.

Initially, staff members were adverse to the idea of such a high level of supervision, but over time it has proven to benefit the staff directly with more manageable children, better organized classrooms and time management. Tori has become the most requested speaker at monthly staff meetings. Our center is fortunate to have Tori living within close proximity to offer hands-on training and help when needed.

Tori's medical knowledge enables our center to discuss with parents medical policies, illness regulations and doctor orders in a manner that ensures parent participation and compliance with center rules and state licensing regulations. When faced with special medical requests Tori is able to explain terms and techniques to staff with non-medical backgrounds in an easily understood manner. Tori's expertise in areas of childcare, including feeding and behavioral management has enabled our center to enact new policies creating a safer environment while continuing to offer great care.

Tori's knowledge of childhood behavior is vast and her methods are rooted in common sense and experience. They are specific and easily understood. Our center has asked Tori to participate in developing behavioral management plans for special needs clients. She has been instrumental in formulating specific techniques that are effective and work quickly. Our staff has been grateful for her input and ideas that meet both the children's and adult's needs.

Daycare center handbooks require regular review. Tori has been instrumental in including new DHS regulations and interpreting new legislation as it is passed. We feel secure in knowing that we can rely on Tori to research new licensing issues that are pertinent to current laws and compliance with state regulations.

Our center also refers parents of children in our care to Tori for assistance with private parenting issues and concerns such as feeding, sleep patterns and behavior at home. This extended, but separate, service has been widely received by parents and takes a great deal of pressure off the administrative staff and reduces liability issues when we refer parents to Tori for specific, non-daycare related advice.

In short, I cannot recommend the Daycare Whisperer enough. All daycare centers would be wise to enlist the services of the Daycare Whisperer. Even if choosing just one area of business, you will quickly find your center using other services once you realize how valuable Tori's expertise and experience are. Our center has been nothing short of thrilled with the time and money Tori has saved us, the injuries and illnesses she has prevented and the favorable response from our staff.

Imagination Station - Clive Iowa

Video Monitoring

With the advent of video cameras in daycare centers, many parents are thrilled with the prospect of being able to watch their child throughout the day, as well as monitor staff action and response. However, as a working parent, it is difficult to concentrate on both the daily tasks of your career and the video feed of your child's daycare center. For parents, Daycare Whisperer consultation services offer monitoring of your child's daycare center room. The Daycare Whisperer reports back to parents any problems or concerns with both the video time stamp and a full written explanation of the events in question.

The Daycare Whisperer has been contracted by daycare center owners to monitor staff in their own centers. As a parent, you, too, can take advantage of this service, allowing you the opportunity of one-on-one viewing.

The Daycare Whisperer will watch your child's room and report back to you their findings. You will receive a report that includes:

- The atmosphere of the room
- How your child interacts with the other children
- How staff handles your child
- Any problems or concerns occurring in the room
- How to approach the center with your concerns to get full resolution

Parent Consultation

Choosing the Right Care Environment

Choosing a daycare for your child can be a daunting task at best. Even the most guarded and prepared parent can find themselves uncertain as to which daycare environment and/or daycare provider might best serve the needs of their family and child. The Daycare Whisperer offers parents an expert opinion regarding the choice of center versus private home care versus nanny care as well as help choosing the right provider/center/nanny.

The Daycare Whisperer has the distinct advantage of understanding the daycare and nanny industry from both the parent and provider perspective. Including the Daycare Whisperer in your family's daycare decisions offers insight from an expert who can translate what a provider is really conveying in conversations with parents.

Choosing Home Daycare

Choosing appropriate, safe and reliable childcare is one of the most important decisions you will ever make. The Daycare Whisperer will assist parents in choosing the best caregiver by providing the following services:

- Interviewing techniques to get real answers from providers to your questions
- Information on what to look for in the daycare environment
- Tips and tricks that enable you to translate what the provider is really saying
- Information regarding any licensing infractions of chosen providers

- Conducting a final phone interview with the provider on your behalf
- Reviewing provider contracts before parents sign
- Feedback with regard to the findings of the Daycare Whisperer

Choosing a Nanny

Employing a nanny might seem like the perfect choice for your family. However, it is important that the right nanny be selected. Tori, the Daycare Whisperer, has the experience and expertise you need while searching for the perfect nanny. Spending more than eight years as a nanny to high profile clients, Tori understands this position from the perspective of the caretaker. Nanny selection services will include:

- Assistance in interviewing nannies
- Bargaining in respect to wages, hours and expectations
- Problem solving
- Strategies nannies employ to manage both children and parents
- Red flags to watch for while the nanny is in your home
- How to maintain a long and successful nanny/client relationship

Daycare Conflict Resolution

The Daycare Whisperer will happily assist in conflict resolution with regard to either a home or center-based daycare. Issues requiring support or resolution services might include:

- Behavioral issues while the child is in attendance at daycare
- Problems with departure or arrival time at daycare
- Refusal to go to daycare

- Pending termination of daycare services due to behavior
- Suspected abuse and/or negligence
- Terminating daycare services on your behalf

Parenting Advice

Being a parent is the hardest job you will ever have. Many parents find that after having their child they need advice and wisdom from seasoned mothers and caregivers. There are many parenting books on the market that share one philosophy or another, but there is nothing more useful or important than specific, personal parenting advice with regard to your individual child and situation. The Daycare Whisperer is an authority on what works and what does not with regard to children, parenting and maintaining harmony at home.

There is an old adage that kids do not come with an instruction manual. Now you have the Daycare Whisperer to help you find and translate that instruction manual your child has been hiding from you! With hundreds of thousands of hours of caring for all types of innate personalities, Tori, the Daycare Whisperer, has likely dealt with your particular parenting dilemma at some point in her three decades of caring for children. And, as a licensed, registered nurse, Tori can give you sound advice regarding all facets of parenting:

- Nutrition and food issues
- Feeding issues including reflux, gagging, selective eaters, food aversions
- Nipple confusion and refusal
- Breast to bottle
- Switching to organics and identifying hidden processed foods
- Managing age appropriate portions and intake
- Bedtime/sleep issues

- Behavior modification
- Behavioral advice and assistance from birth to five years

Expert Witness Services

Tori Fees, the Daycare Whisperer, serves as an expert witness for child abuse, neglect, injury and death cases. She is a registered nurse licensed in Iowa and has been a childcare provider for the last thirty-six years. As a nurse and veteran childcare provider, she has the training and experience and is qualified to review childcare cases and render an opinion. She is familiar with the standards of care for both childcare and special needs childcare. Tori is willing to provide an expert review, deposition, and if necessary, serve as a witness in a trial.

Connect with Tori Fees

Stalk me here:

Visit my website: www.daycarewhisperer.com

Friend me on Facebook: www.facebook.com/daycare.whisperer

Join the Daycare Debate Facebook group:
www.facebook.com/groups/583184301794799/

Join the Child Care Facebook group:
www.facebook.com/groups/142786202558466/

Visit my blog: www.daycare.com/nannyde

Subscribe to my YouTube Channel:
www.youtube.com/channel/UCNqNacjk6G1WS2dt-Qxd4Eg

Made in the USA
Las Vegas, NV
19 June 2021